ECONOMICS
IN ONE LESSON

ECONOMICS
IN ONE LESSON

Fiftieth Anniversary Edition

HENRY HAZLITT

Foreword by
STEVE FORBES

Laissez Faire Books
Baltimore, MD

Fiftieth Anniversary Edtion published by
Laissez Faire Books
808 St. Paul Street
Baltimore, MD. 21202

Published by arrangement with Crown Publishers, Inc.

ISBN 0-930073-19-3 (pb)
ISBN 0-930073-20-7 (hc)

Manufactured in the United States of America

FOREWORD

WE HAVE BEEN INUNDATED LATELY with a barrage of 50th anniversaries of important events — the dropping of the atomic bombs, Iwo Jima, VE and VJ days, Bretton Woods. And with this edition of Henry Hazlitt's best-known work we commemorate another. Five decades have passed since the publication of a book on economics so powerful in its clarity and simplicity that we can declare, without question, it has shaped our world.

With *Economics in One Lesson*, Henry Hazlitt provided a loaded arsenal for those who would do combat with the cloudy and mistaken economic wisdom of the day. In that respect, he is something of a refuter. He addressed every major economic fallacy, all prominently and widely held, and refuted them. He showed why protective tariffs are not protective, why minimum wage laws hurt those they are intended to benefit, and why government attempts to stabilize and fix prices throw them out of whack. And in doing this he advanced the notion that markets freed from government intervention can best serve and improve society.

In a period when the economics undergirding the New Deal were ascendant, Hazlitt emerged as one of the most successful proponents of free markets and one of the most forceful opponents of the Keynesian nostrums dictating U.S. economic policy. From his perch as an editorial writer for *The New York Times* Hazlitt gave the Roosevelt Administration fits. At *The Nation*, where he signed on as literary editor but wrote extensively on economics, he gave his editors similar fits. And, as a regular columnist for *Newsweek* from 1946 to 1966, he helped educate millions about the rudiments of economics and the failures of widespread government intervention. As a sign of the times, today we would be rightly suspicious of any economics writer with that sort of resumé.

Ludwig von Mises called him "our leader." Friedrich Hayek lauded him similarly. H. L. Mencken, not known for lavishing praise on many, revered Hazlitt as "one of the few economists in human history who could really write." But Henry Hazlitt was no economist. At least, not officially. No Ph.D. — or bachelor's degree, for that matter — adorned his walls. Hazlitt's insatiable curiosity about the way the world works led him, self-taught, to an understanding of basic economics astonishing in its breadth and scope.

The extent of Hazlitt's formal schooling was slight, a year and a half at City College in New York. Perhaps the fact that he was relatively unspoiled by the influences of the academy allowed him to gain such profound insight into economics. These insights are on display in *Economics in One Lesson*, which as the name implies, is a primer.

Early in the book Hazlitt treats us to the parable of the Broken Window. As these things go, Hazlitt's Broken Window ranks with Adam Smith's Pin Shop, Bastiat's Petition or Plato's Cave in importance. Society, its lesson goes, fails to see the full consequences of any economic action. While what has happened is clear, what hasn't is seldom considered.

The point of the parable, and of *Economics in One Lesson* generally, is that "the art of economics consists in looking not merely at the immediate but at the longer effects of any act or policy; it consists in tracing the consequences of that policy not merely for one group but for all groups."

Prevailing economic fallacies are the product of the fact that people, being interested parties, usually are unable to discuss economic issues with appropriate objectivity. Demagogues and bad economists exert influence because they peddle ideas not entirely fraudulent: their ideas contain some elements of truth. Much of the fun of reading Hazlitt lies in the objectivity he brings to his subject, and in his attempt to ferret out the entire truth.

Hazlitt shatters the notion that in destruction can be found prosperity, a method of thinking that rejoiced at the economic "progress" made by having to rebuild post-war Europe ("the miracles of production it takes a war to achieve"). Hazlitt elucidates Bastiat's claim that what is not seen is as important as what is. He rails against the phony progress of inflation. He succinctly explains Say's Law, that supply creates its own demand. And this is just in the first few pages.

Reading *Economics in One Lesson* is sheer joy because, as Mencken said, Hazlitt could really write. In the clearest and most lucid terms, the author spills forth his arguments against every major tenet of conventional economic thinking. Wasting nothing, his attacks show why these tenets are wrong in practice and in principle. On the feel-good goal of full employment he notes that we can't have full production without it, but we surely can have full employment without having full production. Our focus must always be on growth and production. Labor-saving machines don't cause unemployment, but actually create more and better jobs. A firm believer in sound money, he writes about how inflation appeals to politicos, why "its siren music has tempted one nation after another down the path to economic disaster."

Sadly, every tenet of the new economics that Hazlitt dispels continues today to rear its head in one form or another. If the crack bureaucrats at the IMF and World Bank had read this book, they would not have recommended policies to Russia that threaten to return it to dictatorship. And the Mexican government might have thought twice about its disastrous peso inflation had the "experts" who recommended it been grounded in the fundamentals of economics.

Hazlitt's work, though, was not without effect. It helped lay the intellectual groundwork for the tremendous economic expansion of the Reagan years. Henry Hazlitt went to his reward in 1993, so it must have been gratifying for him to see the vindication of his ideas in the progress of the 1980s. The ideas in *Economics in One Lesson* have been vindicated in the bookstores as well, selling upward of a million copies since first appearing fifty years ago.

Hazlitt's attack on New Deal thinking was not warmly received by the era's champions. Hazlitt further outraged them by authoring a stunning treatise in 1959, *The Failure of the "New Economics,"* a line-by-line refutation of John Maynard Keynes's *General Theory.* This devastating critique elicited howls of protest from Lord Keynes's defenders. Which likely was anticipated. Hazlitt knew he had struck a nerve. He certainly couldn't have expected acceptance by the establishment and the cultural elite. One indication of the regard in which he is held today by them may be found in the pages of the most recent edition of Bartlett's *Familiar Quotations* (1992). Ronald Reagan, the Great Communicator, received three citations, while *Jimmy Carter* merited six! The *Bartlett's* editor forthrightly admitted he disliked Reagan. Consider poor Hazlitt, arguably the greatest economic journalist of the 20th century. He won't be found in the book. Lord Keynes, by the way, pulled down twelve.

Hazlitt's problem was his greatest virtue. His ideas were—and are, still—quite radical, in the noblest sense of that word. They first go to the root of any proposition, and proceed from there. Henry Hazlitt's dedication to logic and reason explains why his writing has stood the test of fifty years, why we are celebrating this 50th anniversary. May it stand the test of many more.

Steve Forbes
January, 1996

Contents

Preface to the New Edition

THE FIRST EDITION of this book appeared in 1946. Eight translations were made of it, and there were numerous paperback editions. In a paperback of 1961, a new chapter was added on rent control, which had not been specifically considered in the first edition apart from government price-fixing in general. A few statistics and illustrative references were brought up to date.

Otherwise no changes were made until now. The chief reason was that they were not thought necessary. My book was written to emphasize general economic principles, and the penalties of ignoring them—not the harm done by any specific piece of legislation. While my illustrations were based mainly on American experience, the kind of government interventions I deplored had become so internationalized that I seemed to many foreign readers to be particularly describing the economic policies of their own countries.

Nevertheless, the passage of thirty-two years now seems to me to call for extensive revision. In addition to bringing all illustrations and statistics up to date, I have written an entirely new chapter on rent control; the 1961 discussion now seems inadequate. And I have added a new final chapter, "The Lesson After Thirty Years," to show why that lesson is today more desperately needed than ever.

H. H.
Wilton, Conn.
June 1978

Preface to the First Edition

THIS BOOK IS an analysis of economic fallacies that are at last so prevalent that they have almost become a new orthodoxy. The one thing that has prevented this has been their own self-contradictions, which have scattered those who accept the same premises into a hundred different "schools," for the simple reason that it is impossible in matters touching practical life to be consistently wrong. But the difference between one new school and another is merely that one group wakes up earlier than another to the absurdities to which its false premises are driving it, and becomes at that moment inconsistent by either unwittingly abandoning its false premises or accepting conclusions from them less disturbing or fantastic than those that logic would demand.

There is not a major government in the world at this moment, however, whose economic policies are not influenced if they are not almost wholly determined by acceptance of some of these fallacies. Perhaps the shortest and surest way to an understanding of economics is through a dissection of such errors, and particularly of the central error from which they stem. That is the assumption of this volume and of its somewhat ambitious and belligerent title.

The volume is therefore primarily one of exposition. It makes no claim to originality with regard to any of the chief ideas that it expounds. Rather its effort is to show that many of the ideas which now pass for brilliant innovations and advances are in fact mere revivals of ancient errors, and a further proof of the dictum that those who are ignorant of the past are condemned to repeat it.

The present essay itself is, I suppose, unblushingly "classical," "traditional" and "orthodox"; at least these are the epithets with which those whose sophisms are here subjected to analysis will no doubt attempt to dismiss it. But the student whose aim is to attain as much truth as possible will not be frightened by such adjectives. He will not be forever seeking a revolution, a "fresh start," in economic thought. His mind will, of course, be as receptive to new ideas as to old ones; but he will be content to put aside merely restless or exhibitionistic straining for novelty and originality. As Morris R. Cohen has remarked: "The notion that we can dismiss the views of all previous thinkers surely leaves no basis for the hope that our own work will prove of any value to others."* Because this is a work of exposition I have availed myself freely and without detailed acknowledgment (except for rare footnotes and quotations) of the ideas of others. This is inevitable when one writes in a field in which many of the world's finest minds have labored. But my indebtedness to at least three writers is of so specific a nature that I cannot allow it to pass unmentioned. My greatest debt, with respect to the kind of expository framework on which the present argument is hung, is to Frederic Bastiat's essay *Ce qu'on voit et ce qu'on ne voit pas*, now nearly a century old. The present work may, in fact, be regarded as a modernization, extension and generalization of the approach found in Bastiat's pamphlet. My second debt is to Philip Wicksteed: in particular the chapters on wages and the final summary chapter owe much to his *Commonsense of Political Economy*. My third debt is to Ludwig von Mises. Passing over everything that this elementary treatise may owe to his writings in general, my most specific debt is to his exposition of the manner in which the process of monetary inflation is spread.

When analyzing fallacies, I have thought it still less advisable to mention particular names than in giving credit. To do so would have required special justice to each writer criticized, with exact

---

* *Reason and Nature* (1931), p. x.

quotations, account taken of the particular emphasis he places on this point or that, the qualifications he makes, his personal ambiguities, inconsistencies, and so on. I hope, therefore, that no one will be too disappointed at the absence of such names as Karl Marx, Thorstein Veblen, Major Douglas, Lord Keynes, Professor Alvin Hansen and others in these pages. The object of this book is not to expose the special errors of particular writers, but economic errors in their most frequent, widespread or influential form. Fallacies, when they have reached the popular stage, become anonymous anyway. The subtleties or obscurities to be found in the authors most responsible for propagating them are washed off. A doctrine becomes simplified; the sophism that may have been buried in a network of qualifications, ambiguities or mathematical equations stands clear. I hope I shall not be accused of injustice on the ground, therefore, that a fashionable doctrine in the form in which I have presented it is not precisely the doctrine as it has been formulated by Lord Keynes or some other special author. It is the beliefs which politically influential groups hold and which governments act upon that we are interested in here, not the historical origins of those beliefs.

I hope, finally, that I shall be forgiven for making such rare reference to statistics in the following pages. To have tried to present statistical confirmation, in referring to the effects of tariffs, price-fixing, inflation, and the controls over such commodities as coal, rubber and cotton, would have swollen this book much beyond the dimensions contemplated. As a working newspaper man, moreover, I am acutely aware of how quickly statistics become out of date and are superseded by later figures. Those who are interested in specific economic problems are advised to read current "realistic" discussions of them, with statistical documentation: they will not find it difficult to interpret the statistics correctly in the light of the basic principles they have learned.

I have tried to write this book as simply and with as much freedom from technicalities as is consistent with reasonable accuracy, so that it can be fully understood by a reader with no previous acquaintance with economics.

While this book was composed as a unit, three chapters have already appeared as separate articles, and I wish to thank the *New York Times*, the *American Scholar* and the *New Leader* for permission to reprint material originally published in their pages. I am grateful to Professor von Mises for reading the manuscript and for helpful suggestions. Responsibility for the opinions expressed is, of course, entirely my own.

H. H.
New York
March 25, 1946

PART ONE

THE LESSON

CHAPTER I

THE LESSON

ECONOMICS IS HAUNTED by more fallacies than any other study known to man. This is no accident. The inherent difficulties of the subject would be great enough in any case, but they are multiplied a thousandfold by a factor that is insignificant in, say, physics, mathematics or medicine — the special pleading of selfish interests. While every group has certain economic interests identical with those of all groups, every group has also, as we shall see, interests antagonistic to those of all other groups. While certain public policies would in the long run benefit everybody, other policies would benefit one group only at the expense of all other groups. The group that would benefit by such policies, having such a direct interest in them, will argue for them plausibly and persistently. It will hire the best buyable minds to devote their whole time to presenting its case. And it will finally either convince the general public that its case is sound, or so befuddle it that clear thinking on the subject becomes next to impossible.

In addition to these endless pleadings of self-interest, there is a second main factor that spawns new economic fallacies every day. This is the persistent tendency of men to see only the immediate effects of a given policy, or its effects only on a special group, and to neglect to inquire what the long-run effects of that policy will be not only on that special group but on all groups. It is the fallacy of overlooking secondary consequences.

In this lies the whole difference between good economics and bad. The bad economist sees only what immediately strikes the eye; the good economist also looks beyond. The bad economist sees only the direct consequences of a proposed course; the good economist looks also at the longer and indirect consequences. The bad economist sees only what the effect of a given policy has been or will be on one particular group; the good economist inquires also what the effect of the policy will be on all groups.

The distinction may seem obvious. The precaution of looking for all the consequences of a given policy to everyone may seem elementary. Doesn't everybody know, in his personal life, that there are all sorts of indulgences delightful at the moment but disastrous in the end? Doesn't every little boy know that if he eats enough candy he will get sick? Doesn't the fellow who gets drunk know that he will wake up next morning with a ghastly stomach and a horrible head? Doesn't the dipsomaniac know that he is ruining his liver and shortening his life? Doesn't the Don Juan know that he is letting himself in for every sort of risk, from blackmail to disease? Finally, to bring it to the economic though still personal realm, do not the idler and the spendthrift know, even in the midst of their glorious fling, that they are heading for a future of debt and poverty?

Yet when we enter the field of public economics, these elementary truths are ignored. There are men regarded today as brilliant economists, who deprecate saving and recommend squandering on a national scale as the way of economic salvation; and when anyone points to what the consequences of these policies will be in the long run, they reply flippantly, as might the prodigal son of a warning father: "In the long run we are all dead." And such shallow wisecracks pass as devastating epigrams and the ripest wisdom.

But the tragedy is that, on the contrary, we are already suffering the long-run consequences of the policies of the remote or recent past. Today is already the tomorrow which the bad economist yesterday urged us to ignore. The long-run consequences of some economic policies may become evident in a few months. Others may not become evident for several years. Still others may not become evident for decades. But in every case those long-run consequences are contained in the policy as surely as the hen was in the egg, the flower in the seed.

From this aspect, therefore, the whole of economics can be reduced to a single lesson, and that lesson can be reduced to a single sentence. *The art of economics consists in looking not merely at the immediate but at the longer effects of any act or policy; it consists in tracing the consequences of that policy not merely for one group but for all groups.*

2

Nine-tenths of the economic fallacies that are working such dreadful harm in the world today are the result of ignoring this lesson. Those fallacies all stem from one of two central fallacies, or both: that of looking only at the immediate consequences of an act or proposal, and that of looking at the consequences only for a particular group to the neglect of other groups.

It is true, of course, that the opposite error is possible. In considering a policy we ought not to concentrate *only* on its long-run results to the community as a whole. This is the error often made by the classical economists. It resulted in a certain callousness toward the fate of groups that were immediately hurt by policies or developments which proved to be beneficial on net balance and in the long run.

But comparatively few people today make this error; and those few consist mainly of professional economists. The most frequent fallacy by far today, the fallacy that emerges again and again in nearly every conversation that touches on economic affairs, the error of a thousand political speeches, the central sophism of the "new" economics, is to concentrate on the short-run effects of policies on special groups and to ignore or belittle the long-run effects on the community as a whole. The "new" economists flatter themselves that this is a great, almost a revolutionary advance over the methods of the "classical" or "orthodox," economists, because the former take into consideration short-run effects which the latter often ignored. But in themselves ignoring or slighting the long-run effects, they are making the far more serious error. They overlook the woods in their precise and minute examination of particular trees. Their methods and conclusions are often profoundly reactionary. They are sometimes surprised to find themselves in accord with seventeenth-century mercantilism. They fall, in fact, into all the ancient errors (or would, if they were not so inconsistent) that the classical economists, we had hoped, had once and for all got rid of.

3

It is often sadly remarked that the bad economists present their errors to the public better than the good economists present their truths. It is often complained that demagogues can be more plausible in putting forward economic nonsense from the platform than the honest men who try to show what is wrong with it. But the basic reason for this ought not to be mysterious. The reason is that the demagogues and bad economists are presenting half-truths. They are speaking only of the immediate effect of a proposed policy or its effect upon a single group. As far as they go they may often be right. In these cases the answer consists in showing that the proposed policy would also have longer and less desirable effects, or that it could benefit one group only at the expense of all other groups. The answer consists in supplementing and correcting the half-truth with the other half. But to consider all the chief effects of a proposed course on everybody often requires a long, complicated, and dull chain of reasoning. Most of the audience finds this chain of reasoning difficult to follow and soon becomes bored and inattentive. The bad economists rationalize this intellectual debility and laziness by assuring the audience that it need not even attempt to follow the reasoning or judge it on its merits because it is only "classicism" or "laissez faire" or "capitalist apologetics" or whatever other term of abuse may happen to strike them as effective.

We have stated the nature of the lesson, and of the fallacies that stand in its way, in abstract terms. But the lesson will not be driven home, and the fallacies will continue to go unrecognized, unless both are illustrated by examples. Through these examples we can move from the most elementary problems in economics to the most complex and difficult. Through them we can learn to detect and avoid first the crudest and most palpable fallacies and finally some of the most sophisticated and elusive. To that task we shall now proceed.

PART TWO

THE LESSON APPLIED

CHAPTER II

The Broken Window

Let us begin with the simplest illustration possible: let us, emulating Bastiat, choose a broken pane of glass.

A young hoodlum, say, heaves a brick through the window of a baker's shop. The shopkeeper runs out furious, but the boy is gone. A crowd gathers, and begins to stare with quiet satisfaction at the gaping hole in the window and the shattered glass over the bread and pies. After a while the crowd feels the need for philosophic reflection. And several of its members are almost certain to remind each other or the baker that, after all, the misfortune has its bright side. It will make business for some glazier. As they begin to think of this they elaborate upon it. How much does a new plate glass window cost? Two hundred and fifty dollars? That will be quite a sum. After all, if windows were never broken, what would happen to the glass business? Then, of course, the thing is endless. The glazier will have $250 more to spend with other merchants, and these in turn will have $250 more to spend with still other merchants, and so ad infinitum. The smashed window will go on providing money and employment in ever-widening circles. The logical conclusion from all this would be, if the crowd drew it, that the little hoodlum who threw the brick, far from being a public menace, was a public benefactor.

Now let us take another look. The crowd is at least right in its first conclusion. This little act of vandalism will in the first instance mean more business for some glazier. The glazier will be no more unhappy to learn of the incident than an undertaker to learn of a death. But the shopkeeper will be out $250 that he was planning to spend for a new suit. Because he has had to replace a window, he will have to go without the suit (or some equivalent need or luxury). Instead of having a window and $250 he now has merely a window. Or, as he was planning to buy the suit that very afternoon, instead of having both a window and a suit he must be content with the window and no suit. If we think of him as a part of the community, the community has lost a new suit that might otherwise have come into being, and is just that much poorer.

The glazier's gain of business, in short, is merely the tailor's loss of business. No new "employment" has been added. The people in the crowd were thinking only of two parties to the transaction, the baker and the glazier. They had forgotten the potential third party involved, the tailor. They forgot him precisely because he will not now enter the scene. They will see the new window in the next day or two. They will never see the extra suit, precisely because it will never be made. They see only what is immediately visible to the eye.

CHAPTER III

THE BLESSINGS OF DESTRUCTION

SO WE HAVE finished with the broken window. An elementary fallacy. Anybody, one would think, would be able to avoid it after a few moments' thought. Yet the broken-window fallacy, under a hundred disguises, is the most persistent in the history of economics. It is more rampant now than at any time in the past. It is solemnly reaffirmed every day by great captains of industry, by chambers of commerce, by labor union leaders, by editorial writers and newspaper columnists and radio and television commentators, by learned statisticians using the most refined techniques, by professors of economics in our best universities. In their various ways they all dilate upon the advantages of destruction.

Though some of them would disdain to say that there are net benefits in small acts of destruction, they see almost endless benefits in enormous acts of destruction. They tell us how much better off economically we all are in war than in peace. They see "miracles of production" which it requires a war to achieve. And they see a world made prosperous by an enormous "accumulated" or "backed-up" demand. In Europe, after World War II, they joyously counted the houses, the whole cities that had been leveled to the ground and that "had to be replaced." In America they counted the houses that could not be built during the war, the nylon stockings that could not be supplied, the worn-out automobiles and tires, the obsolescent radios and refrigerators. They brought together formidable totals.

It was merely our old friend, the broken-window fallacy, in new clothing, and grown fat beyond recognition. This time it was

13

supported by a whole bundle of related fallacies. It confused *need* with *demand*. The more war destroys, the more it impoverishes, the greater is the postwar need. Indubitably. But need is not demand. Effective economic demand requires not merely need but corresponding purchasing power. The needs of India today are incomparably greater than the needs of America. But its purchasing power, and therefore the "new business" that it can stimulate, are incomparably smaller.

But if we get past this point, there is a chance for another fallacy, and the broken-windowites usually grab it. They think of "purchasing power" merely in terms of money. Now money can be run off by the printing press. As this is being written, in fact, printing money is the world's biggest industry—if the product is measured in monetary terms. But the more money is turned out in this way, the more the value of any given unit of money falls. This falling value can be measured in rising prices of commodities. But as most people are so firmly in the habit of thinking of their wealth and income in terms of money, they consider themselves better off as these monetary totals rise, in spite of the fact that in terms of things they may have less and buy less. Most of the "good" economic results which people at the time attributed to World War II were really owing to wartime inflation. They could have been, and were, produced just as well by an equivalent peacetime inflation. We shall come back to this money illusion later.

Now there is a half-truth in the "backed-up" demand fallacy, just as there was in the broken-window fallacy. The broken window did make more business for the glazier. The destruction of war did make more business for the producers of certain things. The destruction of houses and cities did make more business for the building and construction industries. The inability to produce automobiles, radios, and refrigerators during the war did bring about a cumulative postwar demand *for those particular products*.

To most people this seemed like an increase in total demand, as it partly was *in terms of dollars of lower purchasing power*. But what mainly took place was a *diversion* of demand to these particular products from others. The people of Europe built more new houses than otherwise because they had to. But when they built more houses they had just that much less manpower and productive capacity left over for everything else. When they bought houses they had just that much less purchasing power for something else. Wherever business was increased in one direction, it was (except insofar as productive energies were stimulated by a sense of want and urgency) correspondingly reduced in another.

The war, in short, changed the postwar *direction* of effort; it changed the balance of industries; it changed the structure of industry.

Since World War II ended in Europe, there has been rapid and even spectacular "economic growth" both in countries that were ravaged by war and those that were not. Some of the countries in which there was greatest destruction, such as Germany, have advanced more rapidly than others, such as France, in which there was much less. In part this was because West Germany followed sounder economic policies. In part it was because the desperate need to get back to normal housing and other living conditions stimulated increased efforts. But this does not mean that property destruction is an advantage to the person whose property has been destroyed. No man burns down his own house on the theory that the need to rebuild it will stimulate his energies.

After a war there is normally a stimulation of energies for a time. At the beginning of the famous third chapter of his *History of England*, Macaulay pointed out that:

> No ordinary misfortune, no ordinary misgovernment, will do so much to make a nation wretched as the constant progress of physical knowledge and the constant effort of every man to better himself will do to make a nation prosperous. It has often been found that profuse expenditure, heavy taxation, absurd commercial restriction, corrupt tribunals, disastrous wars, seditions, persecutions, conflagrations, inundations, have not been able to destroy capital so fast as the exertions of private citizens have been able to create it.

No man would want to have his own property destroyed either in war or in peace. What is harmful or disastrous to an individual must be equally harmful or disastrous to the collection of individuals that make up a nation.

Many of the most frequent fallacies in economic reasoning come from the propensity, especially marked today, to think in terms of an abstraction—the collectivity, the "nation"—and to forget or ignore the individuals who make it up and give it meaning. No one could think that the destruction of war was an economic advantage who began by thinking first of all of the people whose property was destroyed.

Those who think that the destruction of war increases total "demand" forget that demand and supply are merely two sides of the same coin. They are the same thing looked at from different directions. Supply creates demand because at bottom it *is* demand. The supply of the thing they make is all that people have, in fact, to offer in exchange for the things they want. In this sense the farmers' supply of wheat constitutes their demand for automobiles and other goods. All this is inherent in the modern division of labor and in an exchange economy.

This fundamental fact, it is true, is obscured for most people (including some reputedly brilliant economists) through such complications as wage payments and the indirect form in which virtually all modern exchanges are made through the medium of money. John Stuart Mill and other classical writers, though they sometimes failed to take sufficient account of the complex consequences resulting from the use of money, at least saw through "the monetary veil" to the underlying realities. To that extent they were in advance of many of their present-day critics, who are befuddled by money rather than instructed by it. Mere inflation—that is, the mere issuance of more money, with the consequence of higher wages and prices—may look like the creation of more demand. But in terms of the actual production and exchange of real things it is not.

It should be obvious that real buying power is wiped out to the same extent as productive power is wiped out. We should not let ourselves be deceived or confused on this point by the effects of monetary inflation in raising prices or "national income" in monetary terms.

It is sometimes said that the Germans or the Japanese had a postwar advantage over the Americans because their old plants, having been destroyed completely by bombs during the war, they could replace them with the most modern plants and equipment and thus produce more efficiently and at lower costs than the Americans with their older and half-obsolete plants and equipment. But if this were really a clear net advantage, Americans could easily offset it by immediately wrecking their old plants, junking all the old equipment. In fact, all manufacturers in all countries could scrap all their old plants and equipment every year and erect new plants and install new equipment.

The simple truth is that there is an optimum rate of replacement, a best time for replacement. It would be an advantage for a manufacturer to have his factory and equipment destroyed by bombs only if the time had arrived when, through deterioration and obsolescence, his plant and equipment had already acquired a null or a negative value and the bombs fell just when he should have called in a wrecking crew or ordered new equipment anyway.

It is true that previous depreciation and obsolescence, if not adequately reflected in his books, may make the destruction of his property less of a disaster, on net balance, than it seems. It is also true that the existence of new plants and equipment speeds up the obsolescence of older plants and equipment. If the owners of the older plant and equipment try to keep using it longer than the period for which it would maximize their profit, then the manufacturers whose plants and equipment were destroyed (if we assume that they had both the will and capital to replace them with new plants and equipment) will reap a comparative advantage or, to speak more accurately, will reduce their comparative loss.

We are brought, in brief, to the conclusion that it is never an advantage to have one's plants destroyed by shells or bombs unless those plants have already become valueless or acquired a negative value by depreciation and obsolescence.

In all this discussion, moreover, we have so far omitted a central consideration. Plants and equipment cannot be replaced by an individual (or a socialist government) unless he or it has acquired or can acquire the savings, the capital accumulation, to make the replacement. But war destroys accumulated capital.

There may be, it is true, offsetting factors. Technological discoveries and advances during a war may, for example, increase individual or national productivity at this point or that, and there may eventually be a net increase in overall productivity. Postwar demand will never reproduce the precise pattern of prewar demand. But such complications should not divert us from recognizing the basic truth that the wanton destruction of anything of real value is always a net loss, a misfortune, or a disaster, and whatever the offsetting considerations in a particular instance, can never be, on net balance, a boon or a blessing.

CHAPTER IV

PUBLIC WORKS MEAN TAXES

THERE IS NO more persistent and influential faith in the world today than the faith in government spending. Everywhere government spending is presented as a panacea for all our economic ills. Is private industry partially stagnant? We can fix it all by government spending. Is there unemployment? That is obviously due to "insufficient private purchasing power." The remedy is just as obvious. All that is necessary is for the government to spend enough to make up the "deficiency."

An enormous literature is based on this fallacy, and, as so often happens with doctrines of this sort, it has become part of an intricate network of fallacies that mutually support each other. We cannot explore that whole network at this point; we shall return to other branches of it later. But we can examine here the mother fallacy that has given birth to this progeny, the main stem of the network.

Everything we get, outside of the free gifts of nature, must in some way be paid for. The world is full of so-called economists who in turn are full of schemes for getting something for nothing. They tell us that the government can spend and spend without taxing at all; that is can continue to pile up debt without ever paying it off because "we owe it to ourselves." We shall return to such extraordinary doctrines at a later point. Here I am afraid that we shall have to be dogmatic, and point out that such pleasant dreams in the past have always been shattered by national insolvency or a runaway inflation. Here we shall have to say simply that all government expenditures must eventually be paid out of the proceeds of taxation; that inflation itself is merely a form, and a particularly vicious form, of taxation.

Having put aside for later consideration the network of fallacies which rest on chronic government borrowing and inflation, we shall take it for granted throughout the present chapter that either immediately or ultimately every dollar of government spending must be raised through a dollar of taxation. Once we look at the matter in this way, the supposed miracles of government spending will appear in another light.

A certain amount of public spending is necessary to perform essential government functions. A certain amount of public works—of streets and roads and bridges and tunnels, of armories and navy yards, of buildings to house legislatures, police and fire departments—is necessary to supply essential public services. With such public works, necessary for their own sake, and defended on that ground alone, I am not here concerned. I am here concerned with public works considered as a means of "providing employment" or of adding wealth to the community that it would not otherwise have had.

A bridge is built. If it is built to meet an insistent public demand, if it solves a traffic problem or a transportation problem otherwise insoluble, if, in short, it is even more necessary to the taxpayers collectively than the things for which they would have individually spent their money had it had not been taxed away from them, there can be no objection. But a bridge built primarily "to provide employment" is a different kind of bridge. When providing employment becomes the end, need becomes a subordinate consideration. "Projects" have to be *invented*. Instead of thinking only of where bridges *must* be built the government spenders begin to ask themselves where bridges *can* be built. Can they think of plausible reasons why an additional bridge should connect Easton and Weston? It soon becomes absolutely essential. Those who doubt the necessity are dismissed as obstructionists and reactionaries.

Two arguments are put forward for the bridge, one of which is mainly heard before it is built, the other of which is mainly heard after it has been completed. The first argument is that it will provide employment. It will provide, say, 500 jobs for a year. The implication is that these are jobs that would not otherwise have come into existence.

This is what is immediately seen. But if we have trained ourselves to look beyond immediate to secondary consequences, and beyond those who are directly benefited by a government project to others who are indirectly affected, a different picture presents itself. It is true that a particular group of bridgeworkers may receive more employment than otherwise. But the bridge has to be paid for out of taxes. For every dollar that is spent on the bridge a dollar will be taken away from taxpayers. If the bridge costs $10 million the taxpayers will lose $10 million. They will have that much taken away from them which they would otherwise have spent on the things they needed most.

Therefore, for every public job created by the bridge project a private job has been destroyed somewhere else. We can see the men employed on the bridge. We can watch them at work. The employment argument of the government spenders becomes vivid, and probably for most people convincing. But there are other things that we do not see, because, alas, they have never been permitted to come into existence. They are the jobs destroyed by the $10 million taken from the taxpayers. All that has happened, at best, is that there has been a *diversion* of jobs because of the project. More bridge builders; fewer automobile workers, television technicians, clothing workers, farmers.

But then we come to the second argument. The bridge exists. It is, let us suppose, a beautiful and not an ugly bridge. It has come into being through the magic of government spending. Where would it have been if the obstructionists and the reactionaries had had their way? There would have been no bridge. The country would have been just that much poorer.

Here again the government spenders have the better of the argument with all those who cannot see beyond the immediate range of their physical eyes. They can see the bridge. But if they have taught themselves to look for indirect as well as direct consequences they can once more see in the eye of imagination the possibilities that have never been allowed to come into existence. They can see the unbuilt homes, the unmade cars and washing machines, the unmade dresses and coats, perhaps the ungrown and unsold foodstuffs. To see these uncreated things requires a kind of imagination that not many people have. We can think of these nonexistent objects once, perhaps, but we cannot keep them before our minds as we can the bridge that we pass every working day. What has happened is merely that one thing has been created instead of others.

2

The same reasoning applies, of course, to every other form of public work. It applies just as well, for example, to the erection, with public funds, of housing for people of low incomes. All that happens is that money is taken away through taxes from families of higher income (and perhaps a little from families of even lower income) to force them to subsidize these selected families with low incomes and enable them to live in better housing for the same rent or for lower rent than previously.

I do not intend to enter here into all the pros and cons of public housing. I am concerned only to point out the error in two of the arguments most frequently put forward in favor of public housing. One is the argument that it "creates employment"; the other that it creates wealth which would not otherwise have been produced. Both of these arguments are false, because they overlook what is lost through taxation. Taxation for public housing destroys as many jobs in other lines as it creates in housing. It also results in unbuilt private homes, in unmade washing machines and refrigerators, and in lack of innumerable other commodities and services.

And none of this is answered by the sort of reply which points out, for example, that public housing does not have to be financed by a lump sum capital appropriation, but merely by annual rent subsidies. This simply means that the cost to the taxpayers is spread over many years instead of being concentrated into one. Such technicalities are irrelevant to the main point.

The great psychological advantage of the public housing advocates is that men are seen at work on the houses when they are going up, and the houses are seen when they are finished. People live in them, and proudly show their friends through the rooms. The jobs destroyed by the taxes for the housing are not seen, nor are the goods and services that were never made. It takes a concentrated effort of thought, and a new effort each time the houses and the happy people in them are seen, to think of the wealth that was not created instead. Is it surprising that the champions of public housing should dismiss this, if it is brought to their attention, as a world of imagination, as the objections of pure theory, while they point to the public housing that exists? As a character in Bernard Shaw's *Saint Joan* replies when told of the theory of Pythagoras that the earth is round and revolves around the sun: "What an utter fool! Couldn't he use his eyes?"

We must apply the same reasoning, once more, to great projects like the Tennessee Valley Authority. Here, because of sheer size, the danger of optical illusion is greater than ever. Here is a mighty dam, a stupendous arc of steel and concrete, "greater than anything that private capital could have built," the fetish of photographers, the heaven of socialists, the most often used symbol of the miracles of public construction, ownership and operation. Here are mighty generators and power houses. Here is a whole region, it is said, lifted to a higher economic level, attracting factories and industries that could not otherwise have existed. And it is all presented, in the panegyrics of its partisans, as a net economic gain without offsets.

We need not go here into the merits of the TVA or public projects like it. But this time we need a special effort of the imagination, which few people seem able to make, to look at the debit side of the ledger. If taxes are taken from individuals and corporations, and spent in one particular section of the country, why should it cause surprise, why should it be regarded as a miracle, if that section becomes comparatively richer? Other sections of the country, we should remember, are then comparatively poorer. The thing so great that "private capital could not have built it" has in fact been built by private capital—the capital that was expropriated in taxes (or, if the money was borrowed, that eventually must be expropriated in taxes). Again we must make an effort of the imagination to see the private power plants, the private homes, the typewriters and television sets that were never allowed to come into existence because of the money that was taken from people all over the country to build the photogenic Norris Dam.

3

I have deliberately chosen the most favorable examples of public spending schemes—that is, those that are most frequently and fervently urged by the government spenders and most highly regarded by the public. I have not spoken of the hundreds of boondoggling projects that are invariably embarked upon the moment the main object is to "give jobs" and "to put people to work." For then the usefulness of the project itself, as we have seen, inevitably becomes a subordinate consideration. Moreover, the more wasteful the work, the more costly in manpower, the better it becomes for the purpose of providing more employment. Under such circumstances it is highly improbable that the projects thought up by the bureaucrats will provide the same net addition to wealth and welfare, per dollar expended, as would have been provided by the taxpayers themselves, if they had been individually permitted to buy or have made what they themselves wanted, instead of being forced to surrender part of their earnings to the state.

CHAPTER V

TAXES DISCOURAGE PRODUCTION

THERE IS A still further factor which makes it improbable that the wealth created by government spending will fully compensate for the wealth destroyed by the taxes imposed to pay for that spending. It is not a simple question, as so often supposed, of taking something out of the nation's right-hand pocket to put into its left-hand pocket. The government spenders tell us, for example, that if the national income is $1,500 billion then federal taxes of $360 billion a year would mean that only 24 percent of the national income is being transferred from private purposes to public purposes.[1] This is to talk as if the country were the same sort of unit of pooled resources as a huge corporation, and as if all that were involved were a mere bookkeeping transaction. The government spenders forget that they are taking the money from A in order to pay it to B. Or rather, they know this very well but while they dilate upon all the benefits of the process to B, and all the wonderful things he will have which he would not have had if the money had not been transferred to him, they forget the effects of the transaction on A. B is seen; A is forgotten.

In our modern world there is never the same percentage of income tax levied on everybody. The great burden of income taxes is imposed on a minor percentage of the nation's income; and these income taxes have to be supplemented by taxes of other kinds. These taxes inevitably affect the actions and incentives of those from whom they are taken. When a corporation loses a hundred cents of every dollar it loses, and is permitted to keep only fifty-two cents of every dollar it gains, and when it cannot adequately offset its years of losses against its years of gains, its policies are affected. It does not expand its operations, or it expands only those attended with a minimum of risk. People who recognize this situation are deterred from starting new enterprises. Thus old employers do not give more employment, or not as much more as they might have; and others decide not to become employers at all. Improved machinery and better-equipped factories come into existence much more slowly than they otherwise would. The result in the long run is that consumers are prevented from getting better and cheaper products to the extent that they otherwise would, and that real wages are held down, compared with what they might have been.

There is a similar effect when personal incomes are taxed 50, 60 or 70 percent. People begin to ask themselves why they should work six, eight or nine months of the entire year for the government, and only six, four or three months for themselves and their families. If they lose the whole dollar when they lose, but can keep only a fraction of it when they win, they decide that it is foolish to take risks with their capital. In addition, the capital available for risk-taking itself shrinks enormously. It is being taxed away before it can be accumulated. In brief, capital to provide new private jobs is first prevented from coming into existence, and the part that does come into existence is then discouraged from starting new enterprises. The government spenders create the very problem of unemployment that they profess to solve.

A certain amount of taxes is of course indispensable to carry on essential government functions. Reasonable taxes for this purpose need not hurt production much. The kind of government services then supplied in return, which among other things safeguard production itself, more than compensate for this. But the larger the percentage of the national income taken by taxes the greater the deterrent to private production and employment. When the total tax burden grows beyond a bearable size, the problem of devising taxes that will not discourage and disrupt production becomes insoluble.

CHAPTER VI

CREDIT DIVERTS PRODUCTION

GOVERNMENT "ENCOURAGEMENT" TO business is sometimes as much to be feared as government hostility. This supposed encouragement often takes the form of a direct grant of government credit or a guarantee of private loans.

The question of government credit can often be complicated, because it involves the possibility of inflation. We shall defer analysis of the effects of inflation of various kinds until a later chapter. Here, for the sake of simplicity, we shall assume that the credit we are discussing is noninflationary. Inflation, as we shall later see, while it complicates the analysis, does not at bottom change the consequences of the policies discussed.

A frequent proposal of this sort in Congress is for more credit to farmers. In the eyes of most congressmen the farmers simply cannot get enough credit. The credit supplied by private mortgage companies, insurance companies or country banks is never "adequate." Congress is always finding new gaps that are not filled by the existing lending institutions, no matter how many of these it has itself already brought into existence. The farmers may have enough long-term credit or enough short-term credit but, it turns out, they have not enough "intermediate" credit; or the interest rate is too high; or the complaint is that private loans are made only to rich and well-established farmers. So new lending institutions and new types of farm loans are piled on top of each other by the legislature.

The faith in all these policies, it will be found, springs from two acts of shortsightedness. One is to look at the matter only from the standpoint of the farmers that borrow. The other is to think only of the first half of the transaction.

Now all loans, in the eyes of honest borrowers, must eventually be repaid. All credit is debt. Proposals for an increased volume of credit, therefore, are merely another name for proposals for an increased burden of debt. They would seem considerably less inviting if they were habitually referred to by the second name instead of by the first.

We need not discuss here the normal loans that are made to farmers through private sources. They consist of mortgages, of installment credits for the purchase of automobiles, refrigerators, TV sets, tractors and other farm machinery, and of bank loans made to carry the farmer along until he is able to harvest and market his crop and get paid for it. Here we need concern ourselves only with loans to farmers either made directly by some government bureau or guaranteed by it.

These loans are of two main types. One is a loan to enable the farmer to hold his crop off the market. This is an especially harmful type, but it will be more convenient to consider it later when we come to the question of government commodity controls. The other is a loan to provide capital—often to set the farmer up in business by enabling him to buy the farm itself or a mule or tractor, or all three.

At first glance the case for this type of loan may seem a strong one. Here is a poor family, it will be said, with no means of livelihood. It is cruel and wasteful to put them on relief. Buy a farm for them; set them up in business; make productive and self-respecting citizens of them; let them add to the total national product and pay the loan off out of what they produce. Or here is a farmer struggling along with primitive methods of production because he has not the capital to buy himself a tractor. Lend him the money for one; let him increase productivity; he can repay the loan out of the proceeds of his increased crops. In that way you not only enrich him and put him on his feet; you enrich the whole community by that much added output. And the loan, concludes the argument, costs the government and the taxpayers less than nothing, because it is "self-liquidating."

Now as a matter of fact that is what happens every day under the institution of private credit. If a man wishes to buy a farm, and has, let us say, only half or a third as much money as the farm costs, a neighbor or a savings bank will lend him the rest in the form of a mortgage on the farm. If he wishes to buy a tractor, the tractor company itself, or a finance company, will allow him to buy it for one-third of the purchase price with the rest to be paid off in installments out of earnings that the tractor itself will help to provide.

But there is a decisive difference between the loans supplied by private lenders and the loans supplied by a government agency. Each private lender risks his own funds. (A banker, it is true, risks the funds of others that have been entrusted to him; but if money is lost he must either make good out of his own funds or be forced out of business.) When people risk their own funds they are usually careful in their investigations to determine the adequacy of the assets pledged and the business acumen and honesty of the borrower.

If the government operated by the same strict standards, there would be no good argument for its entering the field at all. Why do precisely what private agencies already do? But the government almost invariably operates by different standards. The whole argument for its entering the lending business, in fact, is that it will make loans to people who could not get them from private lenders. This is only another way of saying that the government lenders will take risks with other people's money (the taxpayers') that private lenders will not take with their own money. Sometimes, in fact, apologists will freely acknowledge that the percentage of losses will be higher on these government loans than on private loans. But they contend that this will be more than offset by the added production brought into existence by the borrowers who pay back, and even by most of the borrowers who do not pay back.

This argument will seem plausible only as long as we concentrate our attention on the particular borrowers whom the government supplies with funds, and overlook the people whom its plan deprives of funds. For what is really being lent is not money, which is merely the medium of exchange, but capital. (I have already put the reader on notice that we shall postpone to a later point the complications introduced by an inflationary expansion of credit.) What is really being lent, say, is the farm or the tractor itself. Now the number of farms in existence is limited, and so is the production of tractors (assuming, especially, that an economic surplus of tractors is not produced simply at the expense of other things). The farm or tractor that is lent to A cannot be lent to B. The real question is, therefore, whether A or B shall get the farm.

This brings us to the respective merits of A and B, and what each contributes, or is capable of contributing, to production. A, let us say, is the man who would get the farm if the government did not intervene. The local banker or his neighbors know him and know his record. They want to find employment for their funds. They know that he is a good farmer and an honest man who keeps his word. They consider him a good risk. He has already, perhaps, through industry, frugality and foresight, accumulated enough cash to pay a fourth of the price of the farm. They lend him the other three-fourths; and he gets the farm.

There is a strange idea abroad, held by all monetary cranks, that credit is something a banker gives to a man. Credit on the contrary, is something a man already has. He has it, perhaps, because he already has marketable assets of a greater cash value than the loan for which he is asking. Or he has it because his character and past record have earned it. He brings it into the bank with him. That is why the banker makes him the loan. The banker is not giving something for nothing. He feels assured of repayment. He is merely exchanging a more liquid form of asset or credit for a less liquid form. Sometimes he makes a mistake, and then it is not only the banker who suffers, but the whole community; for values which were supposed to be produced by the lender are not produced and resources are wasted.

Now it is to A, let us say, who has credit that the banker would make his loan. But the government goes into the lending business in a charitable frame of mind because, as we say, it is worried about B. B cannot get a mortgage or other loans from private lenders because he does not have credit with them. He has no savings; he has no impressive record as a good farmer; he is perhaps at the moment on relief. Why not, say the advocates of government credit, make him a useful and productive member of society by lending him enough for a farm and a mule or tractor and setting him up in business?

Perhaps in an individual case it may work out all right. But it is obvious that in general the people selected by these government standards will be poorer risks than the people selected by private standards. More money will be lost by loans to them. There will be a much higher percentage of failures among them. They will be less efficient. More resources will be wasted by them. Yet the recipients of government credit will get their farms and tractors at the expense of those who otherwise would have been the recipients of private credit. Because B has a farm, A will be deprived of a farm. A may be squeezed out either because interest rates have gone up as a result of the government operations, or because farm prices have been forced up as a result of them, or because there is no other farm to be had in his neighborhood. In any case, the net result of government credit has not been to increase the amount of wealth produced by the community but to reduce it, because the available real capital (consisting of actual farms, tractors, etc.) has been placed in the hands of the less efficient borrowers rather than in the hands of the more efficient and trustworthy.

2

The case becomes even clearer if we turn from farming to other forms of business. The proposal is frequently made that the government ought to assume the risks that are "too great for private industry." This means that bureaucrats should be permitted to take risks with the taxpayers' money that no one is willing to take with his own.

Such a policy would lead to evils of many different kinds. It would lead to favoritism: to the making of loans to friends, or in return for bribes. It would inevitably lead to scandals. It would lead to recriminations whenever the taxpayers' money was thrown away on enterprises that failed. It would increase the demand for socialism: for, it would properly be asked, if the government is going to bear the risks, why should it not also get the profits? What justification could there possibly be, in fact, for asking the taxpayers to take the risks while permitting private capitalists to keep the profits? (This is precisely, however, as we shall later see, what we already do in the case of "nonrecourse" government loans to farmers.)

But we shall pass over all these evils for the moment, and concentrate on just one consequence of loans of this type. This is that they will waste capital and reduce production. They will throw the available capital into bad or at best dubious projects. They will throw it into the hands of persons who are less competent or less trustworthy than those who would otherwise have got it. For the amount of real capital at any moment (as distinguished from monetary tokens run off on a printing press) is limited. What is put into the hands of B cannot be put into the hands of A.

People want to invest their own capital. But they are cautious. They want to get it back. Most lenders, therefore, investigate any proposal carefully before they risk their own money in it. They weigh the prospect of profits against the chances of loss. They may sometimes make mistakes. But for several reasons they are likely to make fewer mistakes than government lenders. In the first place, the money is either their own or has been voluntarily entrusted to them. In the case of government-lending the money is that of other people, and it has been taken from them, regardless of their personal wish, in taxes. The private money will be invested only where repayment with interest or profit is definitely expected. This is a sign that the persons to whom the money has been lent will be expected to produce things for the market that people actually want. The government money, on the other hand, is likely to be lent for some vague general purpose like "creating employment"; and the more inefficient the work—that is, the greater the volume of employment it requires in relation to the value of the product— the more highly thought of the investment is likely to be.

The private lenders, moreover, are selected by a cruel market test. If they make bad mistakes they lose their money and have no more money to lend. It is only if they have been successful in the past that they have more money to lend in the future. Thus private lenders (except the relatively small proportion that have got their funds through inheritance) are rigidly selected by a process of survival of the fittest. The government lenders, on the other hand, are either those who have passed civil service examinations, and know how to answer hypothetical questions hypothetically, or they are those who can give the most plausible reasons for making loans and the most plausible explanations of why it wasn't their fault that the loans failed. But the net result remains: private loans will utilize existing resources and capital far better than government loans. Government loans will waste far more capital and resources than private loans. Government loans, in short, as compared with private loans, will reduce production, not increase it.

The proposal for government loans to private individuals or projects, in brief, sees B and forgets A. It sees the people into whose hands the capital is put; it forgets those who would otherwise have had it. It sees the project to which capital is granted; it forgets the projects from which capital is thereby withheld. It sees the immediate benefit to one group; it overlooks the losses to other groups, and the net loss to the community as a whole.

The case against government-guaranteed loans and mortgages to private businesses and persons is almost as strong as, though less obvious than, the case against direct government loans and mortgages. The advocates of government-guaranteed mortgages also forget that what is being lent is ultimately real capital, which is limited in supply, and that they are helping identified B at the expense of some unidentified A. Government-guaranteed home mortgages, especially when a negligible down payment or no down payment whatever is required, inevitably mean more bad loans than otherwise. They force the general taxpayer to subsidize the bad risks and to defray the losses. They encourage people to "buy" houses that they cannot really afford. They tend eventually to bring about an oversupply of houses as compared with other things. They temporarily overstimulate building, raise the cost of building for everybody (including the buyers of the homes with the guaranteed mortgages), and may mislead the building industry into an eventually costly overexpansion. In brief, in the long run they do not increase overall national production but encourage malinvestment.

3

We remarked at the beginning of this chapter that government "aid" to business is sometimes as much to be feared as government hostility. This applies as much to government subsidies as to government loans. The government never lends or gives anything to business that it does not take away from business. One often hears New Dealers and other statists boast about the way government "bailed business out" with the Reconstruction Finance Corporation, the Home Owners Loan Corporation and other government agencies in 1932 and later. But the government can give no financial help to business that it does not first or finally take from business. The government's funds all come from taxes. Even the much vaunted "government credit" rests on the assumption that its loans will ultimately be repaid out of the proceeds of taxes. When the government makes loans or subsidies to business, what it does is to tax successful private business in order to support unsuccessful private business. Under certain emergency circumstances there may be a plausible argument for this, the merits of which we need not examine here. But in the long run it does not sound like a paying proposition from the standpoint of the country as a whole. And experience has shown that it isn't.

CHAPTER VII

THE CURSE OF MACHINERY

AMONG THE MOST viable of all economic delusions is the belief that machines on net balance create unemployment. Destroyed a thousand times, it has risen a thousand times out of its own ashes as hardy and vigorous as ever. Whenever there is long-continued mass unemployment, machines get the blame anew. This fallacy is still the basis of many labor union practices. The public tolerates these practices because it either believes at bottom that the unions are right, or is too confused to see just why they are wrong.

The belief that machines cause unemployment, when held with any logical consistency, leads to preposterous conclusions. Not only must we be causing unemployment with every techno-logical improvement we make today, but primitive man must have started causing it with the first efforts he made to save himself from needless toil and sweat.

To go no further back, let us turn to Adam Smith's *Wealth of Nations*, published in 1776. The first chapter of this remarkable book is called "Of the Division of Labor," and on the second page of this first chapter the author tells us that a workman unac-quainted with the use of machinery employed in pin-making "could scarce make one pin a day, and certainly could not make twenty," but with the use of this machinery he can make 4,800 pins a day. So already, alas, in Adam Smith's time, machinery had thrown from 240 to 4,800 pin-makers out of work for every one it kept. In the pin-making industry there was already, if machines merely throw men out of jobs, 99.98 percent unemployment. Could things be blacker?

Things could be blacker, for the Industrial Revolution was just in its infancy. Let us look at some of the incidents and aspects of that revolution. Let us see, for example, what happened in the stocking industry. New stocking frames as they were introduced were destroyed by the handicraft workmen (over 1,000 in a single riot), houses were burned, the inventors were threatened and obliged to flee for their lives, and order was not finally restored until the military had been called out and the leading rioters had been either transported or hanged.

Now it is important to bear in mind that insofar as the rioters were thinking of their own immediate or even longer futures their opposition to the machine was rational. For William Felkin, in his *History of the Machine-Wrought Hosiery Manufactures* (1867), tells us (though the statement seems implausible) that the larger part of the 50,000 English stocking knitters and their families did not fully emerge from the hunger and misery entailed by the introduction of the machine for the next forty years. But insofar as the rioters believed, as most of them undoubtedly did, that the machine was permanently displacing men, they were mistaken, for before the end of the nineteenth century the stocking industry was employing at least a hundred men for every man it employed at the beginning of the century.

Arkwright invented his cotton-spinning machinery in 1760. At that time it was estimated that there were in England 5,200 spinners using spinning wheels, and 2,700 weavers—in all, 7,900 persons engaged in the production of cotton textiles. The introduction of Arkwright's invention was opposed on the ground that it threatened the livelihood of the workers, and the opposition had to be put down by force. Yet in 1787—twenty-seven years after the invention appeared—a parliamentary inquiry showed that the number of persons actually engaged in the spinning and weaving of cotton had risen from 7,900 to 320,000, an increase of 4,400 percent.

If the reader will consult such a book as *Recent Economic Changes*, by David A. Wells, published in 1889, he will find passages that, except for the dates and absolute amounts involved, might have been written by our technophobes of today. Let me quote a few:

> During the ten years from 1870 to 1880, inclusive, the British mercantile marine increased its movement, in the matter of foreign entries and clearances alone, to the extent of 22,000,000 tons . . . yet the number of men who were employed in effecting this great movement had decreased in 1880, as compared with 1870, to the extent of about three thousand (2,990 exactly). What did it? The introduction of steam-hoisting machines and grain elevators upon the wharves and docks, the employment of steam power, etc. . . .
>
> In 1873 Bessemer steel in England, where its price had not been enhanced by protective duties, commanded $80 per ton; in 1886 it was profitably manufactured and sold in the same country for less than $20 per ton. Within the same time the annual production capacity of a Bessemer converter has been increased fourfold, with no increase but rather a diminution of the involved labor.
>
> The power capacity already being exerted by the steam engines of the world in existence and working in the year 1887 has been estimated by the Bureau of Statistics at Berlin as equivalent to that of 200,000,000 horses, representing approximately 1,000,000,000 men; or at least three times the working population of the earth. . . .

One would think that this last figure would have caused Mr. Wells to pause, and wonder why there was any employment left in the world of 1889 at all; but he merely concluded, with restrained pessimism, that "under such circumstances industrial overproduction . . . may become chronic."

In the depression of 1932, the game of blaming unemployment on the machines started all over again. Within a few months the doctrines of a group calling themselves the Technocrats had spread through the country like a forest fire. I shall not weary the reader with a recital of the fantastic figures put forward by this group or with corrections to show what the real facts were. It is enough to say that the Technocrats returned to the error in all its native purity that machines permanently displace men—except that, in their ignorance, they presented this error as a new and revolutionary discovery of their own. It was simply one more illustration of Santayana's aphorism that those who cannot remember the past are condemned to repeat it.

The Technocrats were finally laughed out of existence; but their doctrine, which preceded them, lingers on. It is reflected in hundreds of make-work rules and featherbed practices by labor unions; and these rules and practices are tolerated and even approved because of the confusion on this point in the public mind.

Testifying on behalf of the United States Department of Justice before the Temporary National Economic Committee (better known as the TNEC) in March 1941, Corwin Edwards cited innumerable examples of such practices. The electrical union in New York City was charged with refusal to install electrical equipment made outside of New York State unless the equipment was disassembled and reassembled at the job site. In Houston, Texas, master plumbers and the plumbing union agreed that piping prefabricated for installation would be installed by the union only if the thread were cut off one end of the pipe and new thread were cut at the job site. Various locals of the painters' union imposed restrictions on the use of sprayguns, restrictions in many cases designed merely to make work by requiring the slower process of applying paint with a brush. A local of the teamsters' union required that every truck entering the New York metropolitan area have a local driver in addition to the driver already employed. In various cities the electrical union required that if any temporary light or power was to be used on a construction job there must be a full-time maintenance electrician, who should not be permitted to do any electrical construction work. This rule, according to Mr. Edwards, "often involves the hiring of a man who spends his day reading or playing solitaire and does nothing except throw a switch at the beginning and end of the day."

One could go on to cite such make-work practices in many other fields. In the railroad industry, the unions insist that firemen be employed on types of locomotives that do not need them. In the theaters unions insist on the use of scene shifters even in plays in which no scenery is used. The musicians' union required so-called stand-in musicians or even whole orchestras to be employed in many cases where only phonograph records were needed.

By 1961 there was no sign that the fallacy had died. Not only union leaders but government officials talked solemnly of "automation" as a major cause of unemployment. Automation was discussed as if it were something entirely new in the world. It was in fact merely a new name for continued technological advance and further progress in labor-saving equipment.

2

But the opposition to labor-saving machinery, even today, is not confined to economic illiterates. As late as 1970, a book appeared by a writer so highly regarded that he has since received the Nobel Prize in economics. His book opposed the introduction of labor-saving machines in the underdeveloped countries on the ground that they "decrease the demand for labor"!* The logical conclusion from this would be that the way to maximize jobs is to make all labor as inefficient and unproductive as possible. It implies that the English Luddite rioters, who in the early nineteenth century destroyed stocking frames, steam-power looms, and shearing machines, were after all doing the right thing.

One might pile up mountains of figures to show how wrong were the technophobes of the past. But it would do no good unless we understood clearly *why* they were wrong. For statistics and history are useless in economics unless accompanied by a basic *deductive* understanding of the facts — which means in this case an understanding of why the past consequences of the introduction of machinery and other labor-saving devices *had* to occur. Otherwise the technophobes will assert (as they do in fact assert when you point out to them that the prophecies of their predecessors

---

* Gunnar Myrdal, *The Challenge of World Poverty* (New York: Pantheon Books, 1970), pp. 400–401 and *passim.*

turned out to be absurd): "That may have been all very well in the past but today conditions are fundamentally different; and now we simply cannot afford to develop any more labor-saving machines." Mrs. Eleanor Roosevelt, indeed, in a syndicated newspaper column of September 19, 1945, wrote: "We have reached a point today where labor-saving devices are good only when they do not throw the worker out of his job."

If it were indeed true that the introduction of labor-saving machinery is a cause of constantly mounting unemployment and misery, the logical conclusions to be drawn would be revolutionary, not only in the technical field but for our whole concept of civilization. Not only should we have to regard all further technical progress as a calamity; we should have to regard all past technical progress with equal horror. Every day each of us in his own activity is engaged in trying to reduce the effort it requires to accomplish a given result. Each of us is trying to save his own labor, to economize the means required to achieve his ends. Every employer, small as well as large, seeks constantly to gain his results more economically and efficiently— that is, by saving labor. Every intelligent workman tries to cut down the effort necessary to accomplish his assigned job. The most ambitious of us try tirelessly to increase the results we can achieve in a given number of hours. The technophobes, if they were logical and consistent, would have to dismiss all this progress and ingenuity as not only useless but vicious. Why should freight be carried from Chicago to New York by railroad when we could employ enormously more men, for example, to carry it all on their backs?

Theories as false as this are never held with logical consistency, but they do great harm because they are held at all. Let us, therefore, try to see exactly what happens when technical improvements and labor-saving machinery are introduced. The details will vary in each instance, depending upon the particular conditions that prevail in a given industry or period. But we shall assume an example that involves the main possibilities.

Suppose a clothing manufacturer learns of a machine that will make men's and women's overcoats for half as much labor as previously. He installs the machines and drops half his labor force.

This looks at first glance like a clear loss of employment. But the machine itself required labor to make it; so here, as one offset, are jobs that would not otherwise have existed. The manufacturer, however, would have adopted the machine only if it had either made better suits for half as much labor, or had made the same kind of suits at a smaller cost. If we assume the latter, we cannot assume that the amount of labor to make the machines was as great in terms of payrolls as the amount of labor that the clothing manufacturer hopes to save in the long run by adopting the machine; otherwise there would have been no economy, and he would not have adopted it.

So there is still a net loss of employment to be accounted for. But we should at least keep in mind the real possibility that even the *first* effect of the introduction of labor-saving machinery may be to increase employment on net balance; because it is usually only *in the long run* that the clothing manufacturer expects to save money by adopting the machine: it may take several years for the machine to "pay for itself."

After the machine has produced economies sufficient to offset its cost, the clothing manufacturer has more profits than before. (We shall assume that he merely sells his coats for the same price as his competitors and makes no effort to undersell them.) At this point, it may seem, labor has suffered a net loss of employment, while it is only the manufacturer, the capitalist, who has gained. But it is precisely out of these extra profits that the subsequent social gains must come. The manufacturer must use these extra profits in at least one of three ways, and possibly he will use part of them in all three: (1) he will use the extra profits to expand his operations by buying more machines to make more coats; or (2) he will invest the extra profits in some other industry; or (3) he will spend the extra profits on increasing his own consumption. Whichever of these three courses he takes, he will increase employment.

In other words, the manufacturer, as a result of his economies, has profits that he did not have before. Every dollar of the amount he has saved in direct wages to former coat makers, he now has to pay out in indirect wages to the makers of the new machine, or to the workers in another capital-using industry, or to the makers of a new house or car for himself or for jewelry and furs for his wife. In any case (unless he is a pointless hoarder) he gives indirectly as many jobs as he ceased to give directly.

But the matter does not and cannot rest at this stage. If this enterprising manufacturer effects great economies as compared with his competitors, either he will begin to expand his operations at their expense, or they will start buying the machines too. Again more work will be given to the makers of the machines. But competition and production will then also begin to force down the price of overcoats. There will no longer be as great profits for those who adopt the new machines. The rate of profit of the manufacturers using the new machine will begin to drop, while the manufacturers who have still not adopted the machine may now make no profit at all. The savings, in other words, will begin to be passed along to the buyers of overcoats—to the *consumers*.

But as overcoats are now cheaper, more people will buy them. This means that, though it takes fewer people to make the same number of overcoats as before, more overcoats are now being made than before. If the demand for overcoats is what economists call "elastic"—that is, if a fall in the price of overcoats causes a larger total amount of money to be spent on overcoats than previously—then more people may be employed even in making overcoats than before the new labor-saving machine was introduced. We have already seen how this actually happened historically with stockings and other textiles.

But the new employment does not depend on the elasticity of demand for the particular product involved. Suppose that, though the price of overcoats was almost cut in half—from a former price, say, of $150 to a new price of $100—not a single additional coat was sold. The result would be that while consumers were as well provided with new overcoats as before, each buyer would now have

$50 left over that he would not have had left over before. He will therefore spend this $50 for something else, and so provide increased employment in *other* lines.

In brief, on net balance machines, technological improvements, automation, economies and efficiency do not throw men out of work.

3

Not all inventions and discoveries, of course, are "labor-saving" machines. Some of them, like precision instruments, like nylon, lucite, plywood and plastics of all kinds, simply improve the quality of products. Others, like the telephone or the airplane, perform operations that direct human labor could not perform at all. Still others bring into existence objects and services, such as X-ray machines, radios, TV sets, air-conditioners and computers, that would otherwise not even exist. But in the foregoing illustration we have taken precisely the kind of machine that has been the special object of modern technophobia.

It is possible, of course, to push too far the argument that machines do not on net balance throw men out of work. It is sometimes argued, for example, that machines create more jobs than would otherwise have existed. Under certain conditions this may be true. They can certainly create enormously more jobs *in particular trades*. The eighteenth century figures for the textile industries are a case in point. Their modern counterparts are certainly no less striking. In 1910, 140,000 persons were employed in the United States in the newly created automobile industry. In 1920, as the product was improved and its cost reduced, the industry employed 250,000. In 1930, as this product improvement and cost reduction continued, employment in the industry was 380,000. In 1973 it had risen to 941,000. By 1973, 514,000 people were employed in making aircraft and aircraft parts, and 393,000 were engaged in making electronic components. So it has been in one newly created trade after another, as the invention was improved and the cost reduced.[2]

There is also an absolute sense in which machines may be said to have enormously increased the number of jobs. The population of the world today is four times as great as in the middle of the eighteenth century, before the Industrial Revolution had got well under way. Machines may be said to have given birth to this increased population; for without the machines, the world would not have been able to support it. Three out of every four of us, therefore, may be said to owe not only our jobs but our very lives to machines.

Yet it is a misconception to think of the function or result of machines as primarily one of creating *jobs.* The real result of the machine is to increase *production,* to raise the standard of living, to increase economic welfare. It is no trick to employ everybody, even (or especially) in the most primitive economy. Full employment—very full employment; long, weary, backbreaking employment—is characteristic of precisely the nations that are most retarded industrially. Where full employment already exists, new machines, inventions and discoveries cannot—until there has been time for an increase in population—bring *more* employment. They are likely to bring more *un*employment (but this time I am speaking of *voluntary* and not *in*voluntary unemployment) because people can now afford to work fewer hours, while children and the overaged no longer need to work.

What machines do, to repeat, is to bring an increase in production and an increase in the standard of living. They may do this in either of two ways. They do it by making goods cheaper for consumers (as in our illustration of the overcoats), or they do it by increasing wages because they increase the productivity of the workers. In other words, they either increase money wages or, by reducing prices, they increase the goods and services that the same money wages will buy. Sometimes they do both. What actually happens will depend in large part upon the monetary policy pursued in a country. But in any case, machines, inventions and discoveries increase *real* wages.

A warning is necessary before we leave this subject. It was precisely the great merit of the classical economists that they looked for secondary consequences, that they were concerned with the effects of a given economic policy or development in the long run and on the whole community. But it was also their defect that, in taking the long view and the broad view, they sometimes neglected to take also the short view and the narrow view. They were too often inclined to minimize or to forget altogether the immediate effects of developments on special groups. We have seen, for example, that many of the English stocking knitters suffered real tragedies as a result of the introduction of the new stocking frames, one of the earliest inventions of the Industrial Revolution.

But such facts and their modern counterparts have led some writers to the opposite extreme of looking *only* at the immediate effects on certain groups. Joe Smith is thrown out of a job by the introduction of some new machine. "Keep your eye on Joe Smith," these writers insist. "Never lose track of Joe Smith." But what they then proceed to do is to keep their eyes *only* on Joe Smith, and to forget Tom Jones, who has just got a new job in making the new machine, and Ted Brown, who has just got a job operating one, and Daisy Miller, who can now buy a coat for half what it used to cost her. And because they think only of Joe Smith, they end by advocating reactionary and nonsensical policies.

Yes, we should keep at least one eye on Joe Smith. He has been thrown out of a job by the new machine. Perhaps he can soon get another job, even a better one. But perhaps, also, he has devoted many years of his life to acquiring and improving a special skill for which the market no longer has any use. He has lost this invest-ment in himself, in his old skill, just as his former employer, perhaps, has lost *his* investment in old machines or processes suddenly rendered obsolete. He was a skilled workman, and paid as a skilled workman. Now he has become overnight an unskilled workman again, and can hope, for the present, only for the wages of an unskilled workman, because the one skill he had is no longer needed. We cannot and must not forget Joe Smith. His is one of the personal tragedies that, as we shall see, are incident to nearly all industrial and economic progress.

To ask precisely what course we should follow with Joe Smith — whether we should let him make his own adjustment, give him separation pay or unemployment compensation, put him on relief, or train him at government expense for a new job — would carry us beyond the point that we are here trying to illustrate. The central lesson is that we should try to see *all* the main consequences of any economic policy or development — the immediate effects on special groups, and the long-run effects on all groups.

If we have devoted considerable space to this issue, it is because our conclusions regarding the effects of new machinery, inventions and discoveries on employment, production and welfare are crucial. If we are wrong about these, there are few things in economics about which we are likely to be right.

CHAPTER VIII

SPREAD-THE-WORK SCHEMES

I HAVE REFERRED to various union make-work and featherbed practices. These practices, and the public toleration of them, spring from the same fundamental fallacy as the fear of machines. This is the belief that a more efficient way of doing a thing destroys jobs, and its necessary corollary that a less efficient way of doing it creates them.

Allied to this fallacy is the belief that there is just a fixed amount of work to be done in the world, and that, if we cannot add to this work by thinking up more cumbersome ways of doing it, at least we can think of devices for spreading it around among as large a number of people as possible.

This error lies behind the minute subdivision of labor upon which unions insist. In the building trades in large cities the subdivision is notorious. Bricklayers are not allowed to use stones for a chimney: that is the special work of stonemasons. An electrician cannot rip out a board to fix a connection and put it back again: that is the special job, no matter how simple it may be, of the carpenters. A plumber will not remove or put back a tile incident to fixing a leak in the shower: that is the job of a tile-setter.

Furious "jurisdictional" strikes are fought among unions for the exclusive right to do certain types of borderline jobs. In a statement prepared by the American railroads for the Attorney-General's Committee on Administrative Procedure, the roads gave innumerable examples in which the National Railroad Adjustment Board had decided that each separate operation on the railroad, no matter how minute, such as talking over a telephone or spiking or unspiking a switch, is so far an exclusive property of a particular class of employee that if an employee of another class, in the course of his regular duties, performs such operations he must not only be paid an extra day's wages for doing so, but at the same time the furloughed or unemployed members of the class held to be entitled to perform the operation must be paid a day's wages for not having been called upon to perform it.

It is true that a few persons can profit at the expense of the rest of us from this minute arbitrary subdivision of labor — provided it happens in their case alone. But those who support it as a general practice fail to see that it always raises production costs; that it results on net balance in less work done and in fewer goods produced. The householder who is forced to employ two men to do the work of one has, it is true, given employment to one extra man. But he has just that much less money left over to spend on something that would employ somebody else. Because his bathroom leak has been repaired at double what it should have cost, he decides not to buy the new sweater he wanted. "Labor" is no better off, because a day's employment of an unneeded tile-setter has meant a day's *dis*employment of a sweater knitter or machine handler. The householder, however, is worse off. Instead of having a repaired shower and a sweater, he has the shower and no sweater. And if we count the sweater as part of the national wealth, the country is short one sweater. This symbolizes the net result of the effort to make extra work by arbitrary subdivision of labor.

But there are other schemes for "spreading the work," often put forward by union spokesmen and legislators. The most frequent of these is the proposal to shorten the working week, usually by law. The belief that it would "spread the work" and "give more jobs" was one of the main reasons behind the inclusion of the penalty-overtime provision in the existing Federal Wage-Hour Law. The previous legislation in the states, forbidding the employment of women or minors for more, say, than forty-eight hours a week, was based on the conviction that longer hours were injurious to health and morale. Some of it was based on the belief that longer hours were harmful to efficiency. But the provision in the federal law, that an employer must pay a worker a 50 percent premium above his regular hourly rate of wages for all hours worked in any week above forty, was not based primarily on the belief that forty-five hours a week, say, was injurious either to health or efficiency. It was inserted partly in the hope of boosting the worker's weekly income, and partly in the hope that, by discouraging the employer from taking on anyone regularly for more than forty hours a week, it would force him to employ additional workers instead. At the time of writing this, there are many schemes for "averting unemployment" by enacting a thirty-hour week or a four-day week.

What is the actual effect of such plans, whether enforced by individual unions or by legislation? It will clarify the problem if we consider two cases. The first is a reduction in the standard working week from forty hours to thirty without any change in the hourly rate of pay. The second is a reduction in the working week from forty hours to thirty, but with a sufficient increase in hourly wage rates to maintain the same weekly pay for the individual workers already employed.

Let us take the first case. We assume that the working week is cut from forty hours to thirty, with no change in hourly pay. If there is substantial unemployment when this plan is put into effect, the plan will no doubt provide additional jobs. We cannot assume that it will provide sufficient additional jobs, however, to maintain the same payrolls and the same number of man-hours as before, unless we make the unlikely assumptions that in each industry there has been exactly the same percentage of unemployment and that the new men and women employed are no less efficient at their special tasks on the average than those who had already been employed. But suppose we do make these assumptions. Suppose we do assume that the right number of additional workers of each skill is available, and that the new workers do not raise production costs. What will be the result of reducing the working week from forty hours to thirty (without any increase in hourly pay)?

Ev for counter ag [handwritten margin note]

Though more workers will be employed, each will be working fewer hours, and there will, therefore, be no net increase in man-hours. It is unlikely that there will be any significant increase in production. Total payrolls and "purchasing power" will be no larger. All that will have happened, even under the most favorable assumptions (which would seldom be realized) is that the workers previously employed will subsidize, in effect, the workers previously unemployed. For in order that the new workers will individually receive three-fourths as many dollars a week as the old workers used to receive, the old workers will themselves now individually receive only three-fourths as many dollars a week as previously. It is true that the old workers will now work fewer hours; but this purchase of more leisure at a high price is presumably not a decision they have made for its own sake: it is a sacrifice made to provide *others* with jobs.

The labor union leaders who demand shorter weeks to "spread the work" usually recognize this, and therefore they put the proposal forward in a form in which everyone is supposed to eat his cake and have it too. Reduce the working week from forty hours to thirty, they tell us, to provide more jobs; but compensate for the shorter week by *increasing* the hourly rate of pay by 33.33 percent. The workers employed, say, were previously getting an average of $226 a week for forty hours work; in order that they may still get $226 for only thirty hours work, the hourly rate of pay must be advanced to an average of more than $7.53.

What would be the consequences of such a plan? The first and most obvious consequence would be to raise costs of production. If we assume that the workers, when previously employed for forty hours, were getting less than the level of production costs, prices and profits made possible, then they could have got the hourly increase *without* reducing the length of the working week. They could, in other words, have worked the same number of hours and got their total weekly incomes *increased by one-third*, instead of merely getting, as they are under the new thirty-hour week, the same weekly income as before. But if under the forty-hour week, the workers were already getting as high a wage as the level of production costs and prices made possible (and the very unemployment they are trying to cure may be a sign that they were already getting even more than this), then the increase in production costs as a result of the 33.33 percent increase in hourly wage rates will be much greater than the existing state of prices, production and costs can stand.

The result of the higher wage rate, therefore, will be a much greater unemployment than before. The least efficient firms will be thrown out of business, and the least efficient workers will be thrown out of jobs. Production will be reduced all around the circle. Higher production costs and scarcer supplies will tend to raise prices, so that workers can buy less with the same dollar wages; on the other hand, the increased unemployment will shrink demand and hence tend to lower prices. What ultimately happens to the prices of goods will depend upon what monetary policies are then allowed. But if a policy of monetary inflation is pursued, to enable prices to rise so that the increased hourly wages can be paid, this will merely be a disguised way of reducing *real* wage rates, so that these will return, in terms of the amount of goods they can purchase, to the same real rate as before. The result would then be the same as if the working week had been reduced *without* an increase in hourly wage rates. And the results of that have already been discussed.

The spread-the-work schemes, in brief, rest on the same sort of illusion that we have been considering. The people who support such schemes think only of the employment they might provide for particular persons or groups; they do not stop to consider what their whole effect would be on everybody.

The spread-the-work schemes rest also, as we began by pointing out, on the false assumption that there is just a fixed amount of work to be done. There could be no greater fallacy. There is no limit to the amount of work to be done as long as any human need or wish that work could fill remains unsatisfied. In a modern exchange economy, the most work will be done when prices, costs and wages are in the best relations with each other. What these relations are we shall later consider.

CHAPTER IX

DISBANDING TROOPS
AND BUREAUCRATS

WHEN, AFTER EVERY great war, it is proposed to demobilize the armed forces, there is always a great fear that there will not be enough jobs for these forces and that in consequence they will be unemployed. It is true that, when millions of men are suddenly released, it may require time for private industry to reabsorb them—though what has been chiefly remarkable in the past has been the speed, rather than the slowness, with which this was accomplished. The fears of unemployment arise because people look at only one side of the process.

They see soldiers being turned loose on the labor market. Where is the "purchasing power" going to come from to employ them? If we assume that the public budget is being balanced, the answer is simple. The government will cease to support the soldiers. But the taxpayers will be allowed to retain the funds that were previously taken from them in order to support the soldiers. And the taxpayers will then have additional funds to buy additional goods. Civilian demand, in other words, will be increased, and will give employment to the added labor force represented by the former soldiers.

If the soldiers have been supported by an unbalanced budget—that is, by government borrowing and other forms of deficit financing—the case is somewhat different. But that raises a different question: we shall consider the effects of deficit financing in a later chapter. It is enough to recognize that deficit financing is irrelevant to the point that has just been made; for if we assume that there is any advantage in a budget deficit, then precisely the same budget deficit could be maintained as before by simply reducing taxes by the amount previously spent in supporting the wartime army.

But the demobilization will not leave us economically just where we were before it started. The soldiers previously supported by civilians will not become merely civilians supported by other civilians. They will become self-supporting civilians. If we assume that the men who would otherwise have been retained in the armed forces are no longer needed for defense, then their retention would have been sheer waste. They would have been unproductive. The taxpayers, in return for supporting them, would have got nothing. But now the taxpayers turn over this part of their funds to them as fellow civilians in return for equivalent goods or services. Total national production, the wealth of everybody, is higher.

2

The same reasoning applies to civilian government officials whenever they are retained in excessive numbers and do not perform services for the community reasonably equivalent to the remuneration they receive. Yet whenever any effort is made to cut down the number of unnecessary officeholders the cry is certain to be raised that this action is "deflationary." Would you remove the "purchasing power" from these officials? Would you injure the landlords and tradesmen who depend on that purchasing power? You are simply cutting down "the national income" and helping to bring about or intensify a depression.

Once again the fallacy comes from looking at the effects of this action only on the dismissed officeholders themselves and on the particular tradesmen who depend upon them. Once again it is forgotten that, if these bureaucrats are not retained in office, the taxpayers will be permitted to keep the money that was formerly taken from them for the support of the bureaucrats. Once again it is forgotten that the taxpayers' income and purchasing power go up by at least as much as the income and purchasing power of the former officeholders go down. If the particular shopkeepers who formerly got the business of these bureaucrats lose trade, other shopkeepers elsewhere gain at least as much. Washington is less prosperous, and can, perhaps, support fewer stores; but other towns can support more.

Once again, however, the matter does not end there. The country is not merely as well off without the superfluous office-holders as it would have been had it retained them. It is much better off. For the officeholders must now seek private jobs or set up private business. And the added purchasing power of the taxpayers, as we noted in the case of the soldiers, will encourage this. But the officeholders can take private jobs only by supplying equivalent services to those who provide the jobs — or, rather, to the customers of the employers who provide the jobs. Instead of being parasites, they become productive men and women.

I must insist again that in all this I am not talking of public officeholders whose services are really needed. Necessary police-men, firemen, street cleaners, health officers, judges, legislators and executives perform productive services as important as those of anyone in private industry. They make it possible for private industry to function in an atmosphere of law, order, freedom and peace. But their justification consists in the utility of their services. It does not consist in the "purchasing power" they possess by virtue of being on the public payroll.

This "purchasing power" argument is, when one considers it seriously, fantastic. It could just as well apply to a racketeer or a thief who robs you. After he takes your money he has more purchasing power. He supports with it bars, restaurants, night clubs, tailors, perhaps automobile workers. But for every job his spending provides, your own spending must provide one less, because you have that much less to spend. Just so the taxpayers provide one less job for every job supplied by the spending of officeholders. When your money is taken by a thief, you get nothing in return. When your money is taken through taxes to support needless bureaucrats, precisely the same situation exists. We are lucky, indeed, if the needless bureaucrats are mere easy-going loafers. They are more likely today to be energetic reformers busily discouraging and disrupting production.

When we can find no better argument for the retention of any group of officeholders than that of retaining their purchasing power it is a sign that the time has come to get rid of them.

CHAPTER X

THE FETISH OF FULL EMPLOYMENT

THE ECONOMIC GOAL of any nation, as of any individual, is to get the greatest results with the least effort. The whole economic progress of mankind has consisted in getting more production with the same labor. It is for this reason that men began putting burdens on the backs of mules instead of on their own; that they went on to invent the wheel and the wagon, the railroad and the motor truck. It is for this reason that men used their ingenuity to develop a hundred thousand labor-saving inventions.

All this is so elementary that one would blush to state it if it were not being constantly forgotten by those who coin and circulate the new slogans. Translated into national terms, this first principle means that our real objective is to maximize production. In doing this, full employment—that is, the absence of involuntary idleness—becomes a necessary byproduct. But production is the end, employment merely the means. We cannot continuously have the fullest production without full employment. But we can very easily have full employment without full production.

Primitive tribes are naked, and wretchedly fed and housed, but they do not suffer from unemployment. China and India are incomparably poorer than ourselves, but the main trouble from which they suffer is primitive production methods (which are both a cause and a consequence of a shortage of capital) and not unemployment. Nothing is easier to achieve than full employment, once it is divorced from the goal of full production and taken as an end in itself. Hitler provided full employment with a huge armament program. World War II provided full employment for every nation involved. The slave labor in Germany had full employment. Prisons and chain gangs have full employment. Coercion can always provide full employment.

Yet our legislators do not present Full Production bills in Congress but Full Employment bills. Even committees of businessmen recommend "a President's Commission on Full Employment," not on Full Production, or even on Full Employment *and* Full Production. Everywhere the means is erected into the end, and the end itself is forgotten.

Wages and employment are discussed as if they had no relation to productivity and output. On the assumption that there is only a fixed amount of work to be done, the conclusion is drawn that a thirty-hour week will provide more jobs and will therefore be preferable to a forty-hour week. A hundred make-work practices of labor unions are confusedly tolerated. When a Petrillo threatens to put a radio station out of business unless it employs twice as many musicians as it needs, he is supported by part of the public because he is after all merely trying to create jobs. When we had our WPA, it was considered a mark of genius for the administrators to think of projects that employed the largest number of men in relation to the value of the work performed—in other words, in which labor was least efficient.

It would be far better, if that were the choice—which it isn't—to have maximum production with part of the population supported in idleness by undisguised relief than to provide "full employment" by so many forms of disguised make-work that production is disorganized. The progress of civilization has meant the reduction of employment, not its increase. It is because we have become increasingly wealthy as a nation that we have been able virtually to eliminate child labor, to remove the necessity of work for many of the aged and to make it unnecessary for millions of women to take jobs. A much smaller proportion of the American population needs to work than that, say, of China or of Russia. The real question is not how many millions of jobs there will be in America ten years from now, but how much shall we produce, and what, in consequence, will be our standard of living? The problem of distribution on which all the stress is being put today, is after all more easily solved the more there is to distribute.

We can clarify our thinking if we put our chief emphasis where it belongs—on policies that will maximize production.

CHAPTER XI

WHO'S "PROTECTED" BY TARIFFS?

A MERE RECITAL of the economic policies of governments all over the world is calculated to cause any serious student of economics to throw up his hands in despair. What possible point can there be, he is likely to ask, in discussing refinements and advances in economic theory, when popular thought and the actual policies of governments, certainly in everything connected with international relations, have not yet caught up with Adam Smith? For present-day tariff and trade policies are not only as bad as those in the seventeenth and eighteenth centuries, but incomparably worse. The real reasons for those tariffs and other trade barriers are the same, and the pretended reasons are also the same.

Since *The Wealth of Nations* appeared more than two centuries ago, the case for free trade has been stated thousands of times, but perhaps never with more direct simplicity and force than it was stated in that volume. In general Smith rested his case on one fundamental proposition: "In every country it always is and must be the interest of the great body of the people to buy whatever they want of those who sell it cheapest." "The proposition is so very manifest," Smith continued, "that it seems ridiculous to take any pains to prove it; nor could it ever have been called in question, had not the interested sophistry of merchants and manufacturers confounded the common-sense of mankind."

From another point of view, free trade was considered as one aspect of the specialization of labor:

> It is the maxim of every prudent master of a family, never to attempt to make at home what it will cost him more to make than to buy.

The tailor does not attempt to make his own shoes, but buys them of the shoemaker. The shoemaker does not attempt to make his own clothes, but employs a tailor. The farmer attempts to make neither the one nor the other, but employs those different artificers. All of them find it for their interest to employ their whole industry in a way in which they have some advantage over their neighbors, and to purchase with a part of its produce, or what is the same thing, with the price of a part of it, whatever else they have occasion for. What is prudence in the conduct of every private family can scarce be folly in that of a great kingdom.

But whatever led people to suppose that what was prudence in the conduct of every private family *could* be folly in that of a great kingdom? It was a whole network of fallacies, out of which mankind has still been unable to cut its way. And the chief of them was the central fallacy with which this book is concerned. It was that of considering merely the immediate effects of a tariff on special groups, and neglecting to consider its long run effects on the whole community.

2

An American manufacturer of woolen sweaters goes to Congress or to the State Department and tells the committee or officials concerned that it would be a national disaster for them to remove or reduce the tariff on British sweaters. He now sells his sweaters for $30 each, but English manufacturers could sell their sweaters of the same quality for $25. A duty of $5, therefore, is needed to keep him in business. He is not thinking of himself, of course, but of the thousand men and women he employs, and of the people to whom their spending in turn gives employment. Throw them out of work, and you create unemployment and a fall in purchasing power, which would spread in ever-widening circles. And if he can prove that he really would be forced out of business if the tariff were removed or reduced, his argument against that action is regarded by Congress as conclusive.

But the fallacy comes from looking merely at this manufacturer and his employees, or merely at the American sweater industry. It comes from noticing only the results that are immediately seen, and neglecting the results that are not seen because they are prevented from coming into existence.

The lobbyists for tariff protection are continually putting forward arguments that are not factually correct. But let us assume that the facts in this case are precisely as the sweater manufacturer has stated them. Let us assume that a tariff of $5 a sweater is necessary for him to stay in business and provide employment at sweater-making for his workers.

We have deliberately chosen the most unfavorable example of any for the removal of a tariff. We have not taken an argument for the imposition of a new tariff in order to bring a new industry into existence, but an argument for the retention of a tariff *that has already brought an industry into existence*, and cannot be repealed without hurting somebody.

The tariff is repealed; the manufacturer goes out of business; a thousand workers are laid off; the particular tradesmen whom they patronized are hurt. This is the immediate result that is seen. But there are also results which, while much more difficult to trace, are no less immediate and no less real. For now sweaters that formerly cost retail $30 apiece can be bought for $25. Consumers can now buy the same quality of sweater for less money, or a much better one for the same money. If they buy the same quality of sweater, they not only get the sweater, but they have $5 left over, which they would not have had under the previous conditions, to buy something else. With the $25 that they pay for the imported sweater they help employment—as the American manufacturer no doubt predicted—in the sweater industry in England. With the $5 left over they help employment in any number of other industries in the United States.

But the results do not end there. By buying English sweaters they furnish the English with dollars to buy American goods here. This, in fact (if I may here disregard such complications as fluctuating exchange rates, loans, credits, etc.) is the only way in which the British can eventually make use of these dollars. Because we have permitted the British to sell more to us, they are now able to buy more from us. They are, in fact, eventually *forced* to buy more from us if their dollar balances are not to remain perpetually unused. So as a result of letting in more British goods, we must export more American goods. And though fewer people are now employed in the American sweater industry, more people are employed—and much more efficiently employed—in, say, the American washing-machine or aircraft-building business. American employment on net balance has not gone down, but American and British production on net balance has gone up. Labor in each country is more fully employed in doing just those things that it does best, instead of being forced to do things that it does inefficiently or badly. Consumers in both countries are better off. They are able to buy what they want where they can get it cheapest. American consumers are better provided with sweaters, and British consumers are better provided with washing machines and aircraft.

3

Now let us look at the matter the other way round, and see the effect of imposing a tariff in the first place. Suppose that there had been no tariff on foreign knit goods, that Americans were accustomed to buying foreign sweaters without duty, and that the argument were then put forward that we could *bring a sweater industry into existence* by imposing a duty of $5 on sweaters.

There would be nothing logically wrong with this argument so far as it went. The cost of British sweaters to the American consumer might thereby be forced so high that American manufacturers would find it profitable to enter the sweater business. But American consumers would be forced to subsidize this industry. On every American sweater they bought they would be forced in effect to pay a tax of $5 which would be collected from them in a higher price by the new sweater industry.

Americans would be employed in a sweater industry who had not previously been employed in a sweater industry. That much is true. But there would be no net addition to the country's industry or the country's employment. Because the American consumer had to pay $5 more for the same quality of sweater he would have just that much less left over to buy anything else. He would have to reduce his expenditures by $5 somewhere else. In order that one industry might grow or come into existence, a hundred other industries would have to shrink. In order that 50,000 persons might be employed in a woolen sweater industry, 50,000 fewer persons would be employed elsewhere.

But the new industry would be *visible*. The number of its employees, the capital invested in it, the market value of its product in terms of dollars, could be easily counted. The neighbors could see the sweater workers going to and from the factory every day. The results would be palpable and direct. But the shrinkage of a hundred other industries, the loss of 50,000 other jobs somewhere else, would not be so easily noticed. It would be impossible for even the cleverest statistician to know precisely what the incidence of the loss of other jobs had been—precisely how many men and women had been laid off from each particular industry, precisely how much business each particular industry had lost—because consumers had to pay more for their sweaters. For a loss spread among all the other productive activities of the country would be comparatively minute for each. It would be impossible for anyone to know precisely how each consumer *would* have spent his extra $5 if he had been allowed to retain it. The overwhelming majority of the people, therefore, would probably suffer from the illusion that the new industry had cost us nothing.

4

It is important to notice that the new tariff on sweaters would not raise American wages. To be sure, it would enable Americans to work *in the sweater industry* at approximately the average level of American wages (for workers of their skill), instead of having to compete in that industry at the British level of wages. But there would be no increase of American wages *in general* as a result of the duty; for as we have seen, there would be no net increase in the number of jobs provided, no net increase in the demand for goods, and no increase in labor productivity. Labor productivity would, in fact, be *reduced* as a result of the tariff.

And this brings us to the real effect of a tariff wall. It is not merely that all its visible gains are offset by less obvious but no less real losses. It results, in fact, in a net loss to the country. For contrary to centuries of interested propaganda and disinterested confusion, the tariff *reduces* the American level of wages.

Let us observe more clearly how it does this. We have seen that the added amount which consumers pay for a tariff-protected article leaves them just that much less with which to buy all other articles. There is here no net gain to industry as a whole. But as a result of the artificial barrier erected against foreign goods, American labor, capital and land are deflected from what they can do more efficiently to what they do less efficiently. Therefore, as a result of the tariff wall the average productivity of American labor and capital is reduced.

If we look at it now from the consumer's point of view, we find that he can buy less with his money. Because he has to pay more for sweaters and other protected goods, he can buy less of everything else. The general purchasing power of his income has therefore been reduced. Whether the net effect of the tariff is to lower money wages or to raise money prices will depend upon the monetary policies that are followed. But what is clear is that the tariff—though it may increase wages above what they would have been *in the protected industries*—must on net balance, when *all* occupations are considered, *reduce real wages*—-reduce them, that is to say, compared with what they otherwise would have been.

Only minds corrupted by generations of misleading propaganda can regard this conclusion as paradoxical. What other result could we expect from a policy of deliberately using our resources of capital and manpower in less efficient ways than we know how to use them? What other result could we expect from deliberately erecting artificial obstacles to trade and transportation?

For the erection of tariff walls has the same effect as the erection of real walls. It is significant that the protectionists habitually use the language of warfare. They talk of "repelling an invasion" of foreign products. And the means they suggest in the fiscal field are like those of the battlefield. The tariff barriers that are put up to repel this invasion are like the tank traps, trenches and barbed-wire entanglements created to repel or slow down attempted invasion by a foreign army.

And just as the foreign army is compelled to employ more expensive means to surmount those obstacles—bigger tanks, mine detectors, engineer corps to cut wires, ford streams and build bridges—so more expensive and efficient transportation means must be developed to surmount tariff obstacles. On the one hand, we try to reduce the cost of transportation between England and America, or Canada and the United States, by developing faster and more efficient planes and ships, better roads and bridges, better locomotives and motor trucks. On the other hand, we offset this investment in efficient transportation by a tariff that makes it commercially even more difficult to transport goods than it was before. We make it a dollar cheaper to ship the sweaters, and then increase the tariff by two dollars to prevent the sweaters from being shipped. By reducing the freight that can be profitably carried, we reduce the value of the investment in transport efficiency.

5

The tariff has been described as a means of benefiting the producer at the expense of the consumer. In a sense this is correct. Those who favor it think only of the interests of the producers immediately benefited by the particular duties involved. They forget the interests of the consumers who are immediately injured by being forced to pay these duties. But it is wrong to think of the tariff issue as if it represented a conflict between the interests of producers as a unit against those of consumers as a unit. It is true that the tariff hurts all consumers as such. It is not true that it benefits all producers as such. On the contrary, as we have just seen, it helps the protected producers at the expense of all other American producers, *and particularly of those who have a comparatively large potential export market.*

We can perhaps make this last point clearer by an exaggerated example. Suppose we make our tariff wall so high that it becomes absolutely prohibitive, and no imports come in from the outside world at all. Suppose, as a result of this, that the price of sweaters in America goes up only $5. Then American consumers, because they have to pay $5 more for a sweater, will spend on the average five cents less in each of a hundred other American industries. (The figures are chosen merely to illustrate a principle: there will, of course, be no such symmetrical distribution of the loss; moreover, the sweater industry itself will doubtless be hurt because of protection of still *other* industries. But these complications may be put aside for the moment.)

Now because foreign industries will find their market in America *totally* cut off, they will get no dollar exchange, and therefore they will be *unable to buy any American goods at all.* As a result of this, American industries will suffer in direct proportion to the percentage of their sales previously made abroad. Those that will be most injured, in the first instance, will be such industries as raw cotton producers, copper producers, makers of sewing machines, agricultural machinery, typewriters, commercial airplanes, and so on.

A higher tariff wall, which, however, is not prohibitive, will produce the same kind of results as this, but merely to a smaller degree.

The effect of a tariff, therefore, is to change the *structure* of American production. It changes the number of occupations, the kind of occupations, and the relative size of one industry as compared with another. It makes the industries in which we are comparatively inefficient larger, and the industries in which we are comparatively efficient smaller. Its net effect, therefore, is to reduce American efficiency, as well as to reduce efficiency in the countries with which we would otherwise have traded more largely.

In the long run, notwithstanding the mountains of argument pro and con, a tariff is irrelevant to the question of employment. (True, sudden *changes* in the tariff, either upward or downward, can create temporary unemployment, as they force corresponding changes in the structure of production. Such sudden changes can even cause a depression.) But a tariff is not irrelevant to the question of wages. In the long run it always reduces real wages, because it reduces efficiency, production and wealth.

Thus all the chief tariff fallacies stem from the central fallacy with which this book is concerned. They are the result of looking only at the immediate effects of a single tariff rate on one group of producers, and forgetting the long-run effects both on consumers as a whole and on all other producers.

(I hear some reader asking: "Why not solve this by giving tariff protection to *all* producers?" But the fallacy here is that this cannot help producers uniformly, and cannot help at all domestic producers who already "outsell" foreign producers: these efficient producers must necessarily suffer from the diversion of purchasing power brought about by the tariff.)

6

On the subject of the tariff we must keep in mind one final precaution. It is the same precaution that we found necessary in examining the effects of machinery. It is useless to deny that a tariff does benefit—or at least *can* benefit—*special interests*. True, it benefits them *at the expense of everyone else*. But it does benefit them. If one industry alone could get protection, while its owners and workers enjoyed the benefits of free trade in everything else they bought, that industry would benefit, even on net balance. As an attempt is made to *extend* the tariff blessings, however, even people in the protected industries, both as producers and consumers, begin to suffer from other people's protection, and may finally be worse off even on net balance than if neither they nor anybody else had protection.

But we should not deny, as enthusiastic free traders have so often done, the possibility of these tariff benefits to special groups. We should not pretend, for example, that a reduction of the tariff would help everybody and hurt nobody. It is true that its reduction would help the country on net balance. But *somebody* would be hurt. Groups previously enjoying high protection would be hurt. That in fact is one reason why it is not good to bring such protected interests into existence in the first place. But clarity and candor of thinking compel us to see and acknowledge that some industries are right when they say that a removal of the tariff on their product would throw them out of business and throw their workers (at least temporarily) out of jobs. And if their workers have developed specialized skills, they may even suffer permanently, or until they have at long last learnt equal skills. In tracing the effects of tariffs, as in tracing the effects of machinery, we should endeavor to see *all* the chief effects, in both the short run and the long run, on *all* groups.

As a postscript to this chapter I should add that its argument is not directed against *all* tariffs, including duties collected mainly for revenue, or to keep alive industries needed for war; nor is it directed against all arguments for tariffs. It is merely directed against the fallacy that a tariff on net balance "provides employment," "raises wages," or "protects the American standard of living." It does none of these things; and so far as wages and the standard of living are concerned, it does the precise opposite. But an examination of duties imposed for other purposes would carry us beyond our present subject.

Nor need we here examine the effect of import quotas, exchange controls, bilateralism and other means of reducing, diverting or preventing international trade. Such devices have, in general, the same effects as high or prohibitive tariffs, and often worse effects. They present more complicated issues, but their net results can be traced through the same kind of reasoning that we have just applied to tariff barriers.

CHAPTER XII

THE DRIVE FOR EXPORTS

EXCEEDED ONLY BY the pathological dread of imports that affects all nations is a pathological yearning for exports. Logically, it is true, nothing could be more inconsistent. In the long run imports and exports must equal each other (considering both in the broadest sense, which includes such "invisible" terms as tourist expenditures, ocean freight charges and all other items in the "balance of payments"). It is exports that pay for imports, and vice versa. The greater exports we have, the greater imports we must have, if we ever expect to get paid. The smaller imports we have, the smaller exports we can have. Without imports we can have no exports, for foreigners will have no funds with which to buy our goods. When we decide to cut down our imports, we are in effect deciding also to cut down our exports. When we decide to increase our exports, we are in effect deciding also to increase our imports.

The reason for this is elementary. An American exporter sells his goods to a British importer and is paid in British pounds sterling. But he cannot use British pounds to pay the wages of his workers, to buy his wife's clothes or to buy theater tickets. For all these purposes he needs American dollars. Therefore his British pounds are of no use to him unless he either uses them himself to buy British goods or sells them (through his bank or other agent) to some American importer who wishes to use them to buy British goods. Whichever he does, the transaction cannot be completed until the American exports have been paid for by an equal amount of imports.

The same situation would exist if the transaction had been conducted in terms of American dollars instead of British pounds. The British importer could not pay the American exporter in dollars unless some previous British exporter had built up a credit in dollars here as a result of some previous sale to us. Foreign exchange, in short, is a clearing transaction in which, in America, the dollar debts of foreigners are canceled against their dollar credits. In England, the pound sterling debts of foreigners are canceled against their sterling credits.

There is no reason to go into the technical details of all this, which can be found in any good textbook on foreign exchange. But it should be pointed out that there is nothing inherently mysterious about it (in spite of the mystery in which it is so often wrapped), and that it does not differ essentially from what happens in domestic trade. Each of us must also sell something, even if for most of us it is our own services rather than goods, in order to get the purchasing power to buy. Domestic trade is also conducted in the main by crossing off checks and other claims against each other through clearing houses.

It is true that under the international gold standard discrepancies in balances of imports and exports were sometimes settled by shipments of gold. But they could just as well have been settled by shipments of cotton, steel, whisky, perfume, or any other commodity. The chief difference is that when a gold standard exists the demand for gold is almost indefinitely expansible (partly because it is thought of and accepted as a residual international "money" rather than as just another commodity), and that nations do not put artificial obstacles in the way of receiving gold as they do in the way of receiving almost everything else. (On the other hand, of late years they have taken to putting more obstacles in the way of *exporting* gold than in the way of exporting anything else; but that is another story.)

Now the same people who can be clearheaded and sensible when the subject is one of domestic trade can be incredibly emotional and muddleheaded when it becomes one of foreign trade. In the latter field they can seriously advocate or acquiesce in principles which they would think it insane to apply in domestic business. A typical example is the belief that the government should make huge loans to foreign countries for the sake of increasing our exports, regardless of whether or not these loans are likely to be repaid.

American citizens, of course, should be allowed to lend their own funds abroad at their own risk. The government should put no arbitrary barriers in the way of private lending to countries with which we are at peace. As individuals we should be willing to give generously, for humane reasons alone, to people who are in great distress or in danger of starving. But we ought always to know clearly what we are doing. It is not wise to bestow charity on foreign people under the impression that one is making a hardheaded business transaction purely for one's own selfish purposes. That could only lead to misunderstandings and bad relations later.

Yet among the arguments put forward in favor of huge foreign lending one fallacy is always sure to occupy a prominent place. It runs like this. Even if half (or all) the loans we make to foreign countries turn sour and are not repaid, this nation will still be better off for having made them, because they will give an enormous impetus to our exports.

It should be immediately obvious that if the loans we make to foreign countries to enable them to buy our goods are not repaid, then we are giving the goods away. A nation cannot grow rich by giving goods away. It can only make itself poorer.

No one doubts this proposition when it is applied privately. If an automobile company lends a man $5,000 to buy a car priced at that amount, and the loan is not repaid, the automobile company is not better off because it has "sold" the car. It has simply lost the amount that it cost to make the car. If the car cost $4,000 to make, and only half the loan is repaid, then the company has lost $4,000 minus $2,500, or a net amount of $1,500. It has not made up in trade what it lost in bad loans.[3]

If this proposition is so simple when applied to a private company, why do apparently intelligent people get confused about it when applied to a nation? The reason is that the transaction must then be traced mentally through a few more stages. One group may indeed make gains—while the rest of us take the losses.

It is true, for example, that persons engaged exclusively or chiefly in export business might gain on net balance as a result of bad loans made abroad. The national loss on the transaction would be certain, but it might be distributed in ways difficult to follow. The private lenders would take their losses directly. The losses from government lending would ultimately be paid out of increased taxes imposed on everybody. But there would also be many indirect losses brought about by the effect on the economy of these direct losses.

In the long run business and employment in America would be hurt, not helped, by foreign loans that were not repaid. For every extra dollar that foreign buyers had with which to buy American goods, domestic buyers would ultimately have one dollar less. Businesses that depend on domestic trade would therefore be hurt in the long run as much as export businesses would be helped. Even many concerns that did an export business would be hurt on net balance. American automobile companies, for example, sold about 15 percent of their output in the foreign market in 1975. It would not profit them to sell 20 percent of their output abroad as a result of bad foreign loans if they thereby lost, say, 10 percent of their American sales as the result of added taxes taken from American buyers to make up for the unpaid foreign loans.

None of this means, I repeat, that it is unwise for private investors to make loans abroad, but simply that we cannot get rich by making bad ones.

For the same reasons that it is stupid to give a false stimulation to export trade by making bad loans or outright gifts to foreign countries, it is stupid to give a false stimulation to export trade through export subsidies. An export subsidy is a clear case of giving the foreigner something for nothing, by selling him goods for less than it costs us to make them. It is another case of trying to get rich by giving things away.

In the face of all this, the United States government has been engaged for years in a "foreign economic aid" program the greater part of which has consisted in outright government-to-government gifts of many billions of dollars. Here we are interested in just one aspect of that program—the naive belief of many of its sponsors that this is a clever or even a necessary method of "increasing our exports" and so maintaining prosperity and employment. It is still another form of the delusion that a nation can get rich by giving things away. What conceals the truth from many supporters of the program is that what is directly given away is not the exports themselves but the money with which to buy them. It is possible, therefore, for individual exporters to profit on net balance from the national loss—if their individual profit from the exports is greater than their share of taxes to pay for the program.

Here we have simply one more example of the error of looking only at the immediate effect of a policy on some special group, and of not having the patience or intelligence to trace the long-run effects of the policy on everyone.

If we do trace these long-run effects on everyone, we come to an additional conclusion—the exact opposite of the doctrine that has dominated the thinking of most government officials for centuries. This is, as John Stuart Mill so clearly pointed out, that the real gain of foreign trade to any country lies not in its exports but in its imports. Its consumers are either able to get from abroad commodities at a lower price than they could obtain them for at home, or commodities that they could not get from domestic producers at all. Outstanding examples in the United States are coffee and tea. Collectively considered, the real reason a country needs exports is to pay for its imports.

CHAPTER XIII

"Parity" Prices

SPECIAL INTERESTS, as the history of tariffs reminds us, can think of the most ingenious reasons why they should be the objects of special solicitude. Their spokesmen present a plan in their favor; and it seems at first so absurd that disinterested writers do not trouble to expose it. But the special interests keep on insisting on the scheme. Its enactment would make so much difference to their own immediate welfare that they can afford to hire trained economists and public relations experts to propagate it in their behalf. The public hears the argument so often repeated, and accompanied by such a wealth of imposing statistics, charts, curves and pie-slices, that it is soon taken in. When at last disinterested writers recognize that the danger of the scheme's enactment is real, they are usually too late. They cannot in a few weeks acquaint themselves with the subject as thoroughly as the hired brains who have been devoting their full time to it for years; they are accused of being uninformed, and they have the air of men who presume to dispute axioms.

This general history will do as a history of the idea of "parity" prices for agricultural products. I forget the first day when it made its appearance in a legislative bill; but with the advent of the New Deal in 1933 it had become a definitely established principle, enacted into law; and as year succeeded year, and its absurd corollaries made themselves manifest, they were enacted too.

The argument for parity prices ran roughly like this. Agriculture is the most basic and important of all industries. It must be preserved at all costs. Moreover, the prosperity of everybody else depends upon the prosperity of the farmer. If he does not have the purchasing power to buy the products of industry, industry languishes. This was the cause of the 1929 collapse, or at least of our failure to recover from it. For the prices of farm products dropped violently, while the prices of industrial products dropped very little. The result was that the farmer could not buy industrial products; the city workers were laid off and could not buy farm products, and the depression spread in ever-widening vicious circles. There was only one cure, and it was simple. Bring back the prices of the farmer's products to a parity with the prices of the things the farmer buys. This parity existed in the period from 1909 to 1914, when farmers were prosperous. That price relationship must be restored and preserved perpetually.

It would take too long, and carry us too far from our main point, to examine every absurdity concealed in this plausible statement. There is no sound reason for taking the particular price relationships that prevailed in a particular year or period and regarding them as sacrosanct, or even as necessarily more "normal" than those of any other period. Even if they were "normal" at the time, what reason is there to suppose that these same relationships should be preserved more than sixty years later in spite of the enormous changes in the conditions of production and demand that have taken place in the meantime? The period of 1909 to 1914, as the basis of parity, was not selected at random. In terms of relative prices it was one of the most favorable periods to agriculture in our entire history.

If there had been any sincerity or logic in the idea, it would have been universally extended. If the price relationships between agricultural and industrial products that prevailed from August 1909 to July 1914 ought to be preserved perpetually, why not preserve perpetually the price relationship of every commodity at that time to every other?

When the first edition of this book appeared in 1946, I used the following illustrations of the absurdities to which this would have led:

A Chevrolet six-cylinder touring car cost $2,150 in 1912; an incomparably improved six-cylinder Chevrolet sedan cost $907 in 1942; adjusted for "parity" on the same basis as farm products, however, it would have cost $3,270 in 1942. A pound of aluminum from 1909 to 1913 inclusive averaged 22.5 cents; its price early in 1946 was 14 cents; but at "parity" it would then have cost, instead, 41 cents.

It would be both difficult and debatable to try to bring these two particular comparisons down to date by adjusting not only for the serious inflation (consumer prices have more than tripled) between 1946 and 1978, but also for the qualitative differences in automobiles in the two periods. But this difficulty merely emphasizes the impracticability of the proposal.

After making, in the 1946 edition, the comparison quoted above, I went on to point out that the same type of increase in productivity had in part led also to the lower prices of farm products. "In the five year period 1955 through 1959 an average of 428 pounds of cotton was raised per acre in the United States as compared with an average of 260 pounds in the five-year period 1939 to 1943 and an average of only 188 pounds in the five year 'base' period 1909 to 1913." When these comparisons are brought down to date, they show that the increase in farm productivity has continued, though at a reduced rate. In the five-year period 1968 to 1972, an average of 467 pounds of cotton was raised per acre. Similarly, in the five years 1968 to 1972 an average of 84 bushels of corn per acre was raised compared with an average of only 26.1 bushels in 1935 to 1939, and an average of 31.3 bushels of wheat was raised per acre compared with an average of only 13.2 in the earlier period.

Costs of production have been substantially lowered for farm products by better application of chemical fertilizer, improved strains of seed and increasing mechanization. In the 1946 edition I made the following quotation: "On some large farms which have been completely mechanized and are operated along mass production lines, it requires only one-third to one-fifth the amount of labor to produce the same yields as it did a few years back."[*] Yet all this is ignored by the apostles of "parity" prices.

_____

[*] *New York Times*, January 2, 1946. Of course the acreage restriction plans

The refusal to universalize the principle is not the only evidence that it is not a public-spirited economic plan but merely a device for subsidizing a special interest. Another evidence is that when agricultural prices go *above* parity, or are forced there by government policies, there is no demand on the part of the farm bloc in Congress that such prices be brought *down* to parity, or that the subsidy be to that extent repaid. It is a rule that works only one way.

2

Dismissing all these considerations, let us return to the central fallacy that specially concerns us here. This is the argument that if the farmer gets higher prices for his products he can buy more goods from industry and so make industry prosperous and bring full employment. It does not matter to this argument, of course, whether or not the farmer gets specifically so-called parity prices.

Everything, however, depends on how these higher prices are brought about. If they are the result of a general revival, if they follow from increased prosperity of business, increased industrial production and increased purchasing power of city workers (not brought about by inflation), then they can indeed mean increased prosperity and production not only for the farmers, but for everyone. But what we are discussing is a rise in farm prices brought about by government intervention. This can be done in several ways. The higher price can be forced by mere edict, which is the least workable method. It can be brought about by the government's standing ready to buy all the farm products offered to it at the parity price. It can be brought about by the government's lending to farmers enough money on their crops to enable them

themselves helped to bring about the increased crop yields per acre—first because the acres that farmers took out of cultivation were naturally their least productive; and secondly, because the high support price made it profitable to increase the dosage of fertilizer per acre. Thus the government acreage restriction plans were largely self-defeating.

to hold the crops off the market until parity or a higher price is realized. It can be brought about by the government's enforcing restrictions in the size of crops. It can be brought about, as it often is in practice, by a combination of these methods. For the moment we shall simply assume that, by whatever method, it is in any case brought about.

What is the result? The farmers get higher prices for their crops. In spite of reduced production, say, their "purchasing power" is thereby increased. They are for the time being more prosperous themselves, and they buy more of the products of industry. All this is what is seen by those who look merely at the immediate consequences of policies to the groups directly involved.

But there is another consequence, no less inevitable. Suppose the wheat which would otherwise sell at $2.50 a bushel is pushed up by this policy to $3. 50. The farmer gets $1 a bushel more for wheat. But the city worker, by precisely the same change, *pays* $1 a bushel more for wheat in an increased price of bread. The same thing is true of any other farm product. If the farmer then has $1 more purchasing power to buy industrial products, the city worker has precisely that much less purchasing power to buy industrial products. On net balance industry in general has gained nothing. It loses in city sales precisely as much as it gains in rural sales.

There is of course a change in the incidence of these sales. No doubt the agricultural-implement makers and the mail-order houses do a better business. But the city department stores do a smaller business.

The matter, however, does not end there. The policy results not merely in no net gain, but in a net loss. For it does not mean merely a transfer of purchasing power to the farmer from city consumers, or from the general taxpayer, or from both. It also frequently means a forced cut in the production of farm commodities to bring up the price. This means a destruction of wealth. It means that there is less food to be consumed. How this destruction of wealth is brought about will depend upon the particular method pursued to bring prices up. It may mean the actual physical destruction of what has already been produced, as in the burning of coffee in

Brazil. It may mean a forced restriction of acreage, as in the American AAA plan, or its revival. We shall examine the effect of some of these methods when we come to the broader discussion of government commodity controls.

But here it may be pointed out that when the farmer reduces the production of wheat to get parity, he may indeed get a higher price for each bushel, but he produces and sells fewer bushels. The result is that his income does not go up in proportion to his prices. Even some of the advocates of parity prices recognize this, and use it as an argument to go on to insist upon parity *income* for farmers. But this can only be achieved by a subsidy at the direct expense of taxpayers. To help the farmers, in other words, it merely reduces the purchasing power of city workers and other groups still more.

3

There is one argument for parity prices that should be dealt with before we leave the subject. It is put forward by some of the more sophisticated defenders. "Yes," they will freely admit, "the economic arguments for parity prices are unsound. Such prices are a special privilege. They are an imposition on the consumer. But isn't the tariff an imposition on the farmer? Doesn't he have to pay higher prices on industrial products because of it? It would do no good to place a compensating tariff on farm products because America is a net exporter of farm products. Now the parity-price system is the farmer's equivalent of the tariff. It is the only fair way to even things up."

The farmers that asked for parity prices did have a legitimate complaint. The protective tariff injured them more than they knew. By reducing industrial imports it also reduced American farm exports, because it prevented foreign nations from getting the dollar exchange needed for taking our agricultural products. And it provoked retaliatory tariffs in other countries. Nonetheless, the argument we have just quoted will not stand examination. It is wrong even in its implied statement of the facts. There is no *general* tariff on all "industrial" products or on all nonfarm products. There are scores of domestic industries or of exporting industries that have no tariff protection. If the city worker has to pay a higher price for woolen blankets or overcoats because of a tariff, is he "compensated" by having to pay a higher price also for cotton clothing and for foodstuffs? Or is he merely being robbed twice?

Let us even it all out, say some, by giving equal "protection" to everybody. But that is insoluble and impossible. Even if we assume that the problem could be solved technically—a tariff for A, an industrialist subject to foreign competition; a subsidy for B, an industrialist who exports his product—it would be impossible to protect or to subsidize everybody "fairly" or equally. We should have to give everyone the same percentage (or should it be the same dollar amount?) of tariff protection or subsidy, and we could never be sure when we were duplicating payments to some groups or leaving gaps with others.

But suppose we could solve this fantastic problem? What would be the point? Who gains when everyone equally subsidizes everyone else? What is the profit when everyone loses in added taxes precisely what he gains by his subsidy or his protection? We should merely have added an army of needless bureaucrats to carry out the program, with all of them lost to production.

We could solve the matter simply, on the other hand, by ending both the parity-price system and the protective-tariff system. Meanwhile they do not, in combination, even out anything. The joint system means merely that Farmer A and Industrialist B both profit at the expense of Forgotten Man C.

So the alleged benefits of still another scheme evaporate as soon as we trace not only its immediate effects on a special group but its long-run effects on everyone.

CHAPTER XIV

SAVING THE X INDUSTRY

THE LOBBIES OF Congress are crowded with representatives of
the X industry. The X industry is sick. The X industry is dying. It
must be saved. It can be saved only by a tariff, by higher prices, or
by a subsidy. If it is allowed to die, workers will be thrown on the
streets. Their landlords, grocers, butchers, clothing stores and local
motion pictures will lose business, and depression will spread in
ever-widening circles. But if the X industry, by prompt action of
Congress, is *saved*—ah then! It will buy equipment from other
industries; more men will be employed; they will give more
business to the butchers, bakers and neon-light makers, and then
it is prosperity that will spread in ever-widening circles.

It is obvious that this is merely a generalized form of the case
we have just been considering. There the X industry was agriculture. But there is an endless number of X industries. Two of the
most notable examples have been the coal and silver industries.
To "save silver" Congress did immense harm. One of the arguments for the rescue plan was that it would help "the East." One
of its actual results was to cause deflation in China, which had
been on a silver basis, and to force China off that basis. The United
States Treasury was compelled to acquire, at ridiculous prices far
above the market level, hoards of unnecessary silver, and to store
it in vaults. The essential political aims of the "silver senators"
could have been as well achieved, at a fraction of the harm and
cost, by the payment of a frank subsidy to the mine owners or to
their workers; but Congress and the country would never have
approved a naked steal of this sort unaccompanied by the ideologi-

cal flim-flam regarding "silver's essential role in the national currency."

To save the coal industry Congress passed the Guffey Act, under which the owners of coal mines were not only permitted, but compelled, to conspire together not to sell below certain minimum prices fixed by the government. Though Congress had started out to fix "the" price of coal, the government soon found itself (because of different sizes, thousands of mines, and shipments to thousands of different destinations by rail, truck, ship and barge) fixing 350,000 separate prices for coal![*] One effect of this attempt to keep coal prices above the competitive market level was to accelerate the tendency toward the substitution by consumers of other sources of power or heat—such as oil, natural gas and hydroelectric energy. Today we find the government trying to force conversion from oil consumption back to coal.

2

Our aim here is not to trace all the results that followed historically from efforts to save particular industries, but to trace a few of the chief results that must necessarily follow from efforts to save an industry.

It may be argued that a given industry must be created or preserved for military reasons. It may be argued that a given industry is being ruined by taxes or wage rates disproportionate to those of other industries; or that, if a public utility, it is being forced to operate at rates or charges to the public that do not permit an adequate profit margin. Such arguments may or may not be justified in a particular case. We are not concerned with them here. We are concerned only with a single argument for saving the X industry—that if it is allowed to shrink in size or perish through

---

* Testimony of Dan H. Wheeler, director of the Bituminous Coal Division. Hearings on extension of the Bituminous Coal Act of 1937.

the forces of free competition (always called by spokesmen for the industry in such cases laissez-faire, anarchic, cutthroat, dog-eat-dog, law-of-the-jungle competition) it will pull down the general economy with it, and that if it is artificially kept alive it will help everybody else.

What we are talking about here is nothing else but a generalized case of the argument put forward for parity prices for farm products or for tariff protection for any number of X industries. The argument against artificially higher prices applies, of course, not only to farm products but to any product, just as the reasons we have found for opposing tariff protection for one industry apply to any other.

But there are always any number of schemes for saving X industries. There are two main types of such proposals in addition to those we have already considered, and we shall take a brief glance at them. One is to contend that the X industry is already "overcrowded," and to try to prevent other firms or workers from getting into it. The other is to argue that the X industry needs to be supported by a direct subsidy from the government.

Now if the X industry is really overcrowded as compared with other industries it will not need any coercive legislation to keep out new capital or new workers. New capital does not rush into industries that are obviously dying. Investors do not eagerly seek the industries that present the highest risks of loss combined with the lowest returns. Nor do workers, when they have any better alternative, go into industries where the wages are lowest and the prospects for steady employment least promising.

If new capital and new labor are forcibly kept out of the X industry, however, either by monopolies, cartels, union policy or legislation, it deprives this capital and labor of liberty of choice. It forces investors to place their money where the returns seem less promising to them than in the X industry. It forces workers into industries with even lower wages and prospects than they could find in the allegedly sick X industry. It means, in short, that both capital and labor are less efficiently employed than they would be if they were permitted to make their own free choices. It means, therefore, a lowering of production which must reflect itself in a lower average living standard.

That lower living standard will be brought about either by lower average money wages than would otherwise prevail or by higher average living costs, or by a combination of both. (The exact result would depend upon the accompanying monetary policy.) By these restrictive policies wages and capital returns might indeed be kept higher than otherwise within the X industry itself; but wages and capital returns in other industries would be forced down lower than otherwise. The X industry would benefit only at the expense of the A, B and C industries.

3

Similar results would follow any attempt to save the X industry by a direct subsidy out of the public till. This would be nothing more than a transfer of wealth or income to the X industry. The taxpayers would lose precisely as much as the people in the X industry gained. The great advantage of a subsidy, indeed, from the standpoint of the public, is that it makes this fact so clear. There is far less opportunity for the intellectual obfuscation that accompanies arguments for tariffs, minimum-price fixing or monopolistic exclusion.

It is obvious in the case of a subsidy that the taxpayers must lose precisely as much as the X industry gains. It should be equally clear that, as a consequence, other industries must lose what the X industry gains. They must pay part of the taxes that are used to support the X industry. And customers, because they are taxed to support the X industry, will have that much less income left with which to buy other things. The result must be that other industries on the average must be smaller than otherwise in order that the X industry may be larger.

But the result of this subsidy is not merely that there has been a transfer of wealth or income, or that other industries have shrunk in the aggregate as much as the X industry has expanded. The result is also (and this is where the net loss comes in to the nation considered as a unit) that capital and labor are driven out of industries in which they are more efficiently employed to be diverted to an industry in which they are less efficiently employed. Less wealth is created. The average standard of living is lowered compared with what it would have been.

4

These results are virtually inherent, in fact, in the very arguments put forward to subsidize the X industry. The X industry is shrinking or dying by the contention of its friends. Why, it may be asked, should it be kept alive by artificial respiration? The idea that an expanding economy implies that *all* industries must be simultaneously expanding is a profound error. In order that new industries may grow fast enough it is usually necessary that some old industries should be allowed to shrink or die. In doing this they help to release the necessary capital and labor for the new industries. If we had tried to keep the horse-and-buggy trade artificially alive we should have slowed down the growth of the automobile industry and all the trades dependent on it. We should have lowered the production of wealth and retarded economic and scientific progress.

We do the same thing, however, when we try to prevent any industry from dying in order to protect the labor already trained or the capital already invested in it. Paradoxical as it may seem to some, it is just as necessary to the health of a dynamic economy that dying industries be allowed to die as that growing industries be allowed to grow. The first process is essential to the second. It is as foolish to try to preserve obsolescent industries as to try to preserve obsolescent methods of production: this is often, in fact, merely two ways of describing the same thing. Improved methods of production must constantly supplant obsolete methods, if both old needs and new wants are to be filled by better commodities and better means.

CHAPTER XV

HOW THE PRICE SYSTEM WORKS

THE WHOLE ARGUMENT of this book may be summed up in the statement that in studying the effects of any given economic proposal we must trace not merely the immediate results but the results in the long run, not merely the primary consequences but the secondary consequences, and not merely the effects on some special group but the effects on everyone. It follows that it is foolish and misleading to concentrate our attention merely on some special point—to examine, for example, merely what happens in one industry without considering what happens in all. But it is precisely from the persistent and lazy habit of thinking only of some particular industry or process in isolation that the major fallacies of economics stem. These fallacies pervade not merely the arguments of the hired spokesmen of special interests, but the arguments even of some economists who pass as profound.

It is on the fallacy of isolation, at bottom, that the "production-for-use-and-not-for-profit" school is based, with its attack on the allegedly vicious "price system." The problem of production, say the adherents of this school, is solved. (This resounding error, as we shall see, is also the starting point of most currency cranks and share-the-wealth charlatans.) The scientists, the efficiency experts, the engineers, the technicians, have solved it. They could turn out almost anything you cared to mention in huge and practically unlimited amounts. But, alas, the world is not ruled by the engineers, thinking only of production, but by the businessmen, thinking only of profit. The businessmen give their orders to the engineers, instead of vice versa. These businessmen will turn out any object as long as there is a profit in doing so, but the moment there is no longer a profit in making that article, the wicked businessmen will stop making it, though many people's wants are unsatisfied, and the world is crying for more goods.

There are so many fallacies in this view that they cannot all be disentangled at once. But the central error, as we have hinted, comes from looking at only one industry, or even at several industries in turn, as if each of them existed in isolation. Each of them in fact exists in relation to all the others, and every important decision made in it is affected by and affects the decisions made in all the others.

We can understand this better if we understand the basic problem that business collectively has to solve. To simplify this as much as possible, let us consider the problem that confronts a Robinson Crusoe on his desert island. His wants at first seem endless. He is soaked with rain; he shivers from cold; he suffers from hunger and thirst. He needs everything: drinking water, food, a roof over his head, protection from animals, a fire, a soft place to lie down. It is impossible for him to satisfy all these needs at once; he has not the time, energy or resources. He must attend immediately to the most pressing need. He suffers most, say, from thirst. He hollows out a place in the sand to collect rain water, or builds some crude receptacle. When he has provided for only a small water supply, however, he must turn to finding food before he tries to improve this. He can try to fish; but to do this he needs either a hook and line, or a net, and he must set to work on these. But everything he does delays or prevents him from doing something else only a little less urgent. He is faced constantly by the problem of *alternative* applications of his time and labor.

A Swiss Family Robinson, perhaps, finds this problem a little easier to solve. It has more mouths to feed, but it also has more hands to work for them. It can practice division and specialization of labor. The father hunts; the mother prepares the food; the children collect firewood. But even the family cannot afford to have one member of it doing endlessly the same thing, regardless of the relative urgency of the common need he supplies and the urgency of other needs still unfilled. When the children have gathered a certain pile of firewood, they cannot be used simply to increase the pile. It is soon time for one of them to be sent, say, for more water. The family too has the constant problem of choosing among *alternative* applications of labor, and, if it is lucky enough to have acquired guns, fishing tackle, a boat, axes, saws and so on, of choosing among alternative applications of labor and capital. It would be considered unspeakably silly for the wood-gathering member of the family to complain that they could gather more firewood if his brother helped him all day, instead of getting the fish that were needed for the family dinner. It is recognized clearly in the case of an isolated individual or family that one occupation can expand *only at the expense of all other occupations.*

Elementary illustrations like this are sometimes ridiculed as "Crusoe economics." Unfortunately, they are ridiculed most by those who most need them, who fail to understand the particular principle illustrated even in this simple form, or who lose track of that principle completely when they come to examine the bewildering complications of a great modern economic society.

2

Let us now turn to such a society. How is the problem of alternative applications of labor and capital, to meet thousands of different needs and wants of different urgencies, solved in such a society? It is solved precisely through the price system. It is solved through the constantly changing interrelationships of costs of production, prices and profits.

Prices are fixed through the relationship of supply and demand and in turn affect supply and demand. When people want more of an article, they offer more for it. The price goes up. This increases the profits of those who make the article. Because it is now more profitable to make that article than others, the people already in the business expand their production of it, and more people are attracted to the business. This increased supply then reduces the price and reduces the profit margin, until the profit margin on that article once more falls to the general level of profits (relative risks considered) in other industries. Or the demand for that article may fall; or the supply of it may be increased to such a point that its price drops to a level where there is less profit in making it than in making other articles; or perhaps there is an actual loss in making it. In this case the "marginal" producers, that is, the producers who are least efficient, or whose costs of production are highest, will be driven out of business altogether. The product will now be made only by the more efficient producers who operate on lower costs. The supply of that commodity will also drop, or will at least cease to expand.

This process is the origin of the belief that prices are determined by costs of production. The doctrine, stated in this form, is not true. Prices are determined by supply and demand, and demand is determined by how intensely people want a commodity and what they have to offer in exchange for it. It is true that supply is in part determined by costs of production. What a commodity *has* cost to produce in the past cannot determine its value. That will depend on the *present* relationship of supply and demand. But the expectations of businessmen concerning what a commodity *will* cost to produce in the future, and what its future price will be, will determine how much of it will be made. This will affect future supply. There is therefore a constant tendency for the price of a commodity and its marginal cost of production to *equal* each other, but not because that marginal cost of production directly determines the price.

The private enterprise system, then, might be compared to thousands of machines, each regulated by its own quasi-automatic governor, yet with these machines and their governors all interconnected and influencing each other, so that they act in effect like one great machine. Most of us must have noticed the automatic "governor" on a steam engine. It usually consists of two balls or weights which work by centrifugal force. As the speed of the engine increases, these balls fly away from the rod to which they are attached and so automatically narrow or close off a throttle valve which regulates the intake of steam and thus slows down the engine. If the engine goes too slowly, on the other hand, the balls drop, widen the throttle valve, and increase the engine's speed. Thus every departure from the desired speed itself sets in motion the forces that tend to correct that departure.

It is precisely in this way that the relative supply of thousands of different commodities is regulated under the system of competitive private enterprise. When people want more of a commodity, their competitive bidding raises its price. This increases the profits of the producers who make that product. This stimulates them to increase their production. It leads others to stop making some of the products they previously made, and turn to making the product that offers them the better return. But this increases the supply of that commodity at the same time that it reduces the supply of some other commodities. The price of that product therefore falls in relation to the price of other products, and the stimulus to the relative increase in its production disappears.

In the same way, if the demand falls off for some product, its price and the profit in making it go lower, and its production declines.

It is this last development that scandalizes those who do not understand the "price system" they denounce. They accuse it of creating scarcity. Why, they ask indignantly, should manufacturers cut off the production of shoes at the point where it becomes unprofitable to produce any more? Why should they be guided merely by their own profits? Why should they be guided by the market? Why do they not produce shoes to the "full capacity of modern technical processes"? The price system and private enterprise, conclude the "production-for-use" philosophers, are merely a form of "scarcity economics."

These questions and conclusions stem from the fallacy of looking at one industry in isolation, of looking at the tree and ignoring the forest. Up to a certain point it is necessary to produce shoes. But it is also necessary to produce coats, shirts, trousers, homes, plows, shovels, factories, bridges, milk and bread. It would be idiotic to go on piling up mountains of surplus shoes, simply because we could do it, while hundreds of more urgent needs went unfilled.

Now, in an economy in equilibrium, a given industry can expand *only at the expense of other industries*. For at any moment the factors of production are limited. One industry can be expanded only by *diverting* to it labor, land and capital that would otherwise be employed in other industries. And when a given industry shrinks, or stops expanding its output, it does not necessarily mean that there has been any *net* decline in aggregate production. The shrinkage at that point may have merely *released* labor and capital to *permit the expansion of other industries*. It is erroneous to conclude, therefore, that a shrinkage of production in one line necessarily means a shrinkage in *total* production.

Everything, in short, is produced at the expense of forgoing something else. Costs of production themselves, in fact, might be defined as the things that are given up (the leisure and pleasures, the raw materials with alternative potential uses) in order to create the thing that is made.

It follows that it is just as essential for the health of a dynamic economy that dying industries should be allowed to die as that growing industries should be allowed to grow. For the dying industries absorb labor and capital that should be released for the growing industries. It is only the much vilified price system that solves the enormously complicated problem of deciding precisely how much of tens of thousands of different commodities and services should be produced in relation to each other. These otherwise bewildering equations are solved quasi-automatically by the system of prices, profits and costs. They are solved by this system incomparably better than any group of bureaucrats could solve them. For they are solved by a system under which each consumer makes his own demand and casts a fresh vote, or a dozen fresh votes, every day; whereas bureaucrats would try to solve it by having made for the consumers, not what the consumers themselves wanted, but what the bureaucrats decided was good for them.

Yet though the bureaucrats do not understand the quasi-automatic system of the market, they are always disturbed by it. They are always trying to improve it or correct it, usually in the interests of some wailing pressure group. What some of the results of their intervention are, we shall examine in succeeding chapters.

CHAPTER XVI

"Stabilizing" Commodities

ATTEMPTS TO LIFT the prices of particular commodities permanently above their natural market levels have failed so often, so disastrously and so notoriously that sophisticated pressure groups, and the bureaucrats upon whom they apply the pressure, seldom openly avow that aim. Their stated aims, particularly when they are first proposing that the government intervene, are usually more modest, and more plausible.

They have no wish, they declare, to raise the price of commodity X permanently above its natural level. That, they concede, would be unfair to consumers. But it is *now* obviously selling far *below* its natural level. The producers cannot make a living. Unless we act promptly, they will be thrown out of business. Then there will be a real scarcity, and consumers will have to pay exorbitant prices for the commodity. The apparent bargains that the consumers are now getting will cost them dear in the end. For the present "temporary" low price cannot last. But we cannot afford to wait for so-called natural market forces, or for the "blind" law of supply and demand, to correct the situation. For by that time the producers will be ruined and a great scarcity will be upon us. The government must *act*. All that we really want to do is to correct these violent, senseless *fluctuations* in price. We are not trying to *boost* the price; we are only trying to *stabilize* it.

There are several methods by which it is commonly proposed to do this. One of the most frequent is government loans to farmers to enable them to hold their crops off the market.

Such loans are urged in Congress for reasons that seem very plausible to most listeners. They are told that the farmers' crops are all dumped on the market at once, at harvest time; that this is precisely the time when prices are lowest, and that speculators take advantage of this to buy the crops themselves and hold them for higher prices when food gets scarcer again. Thus it is urged that the farmers suffer, and that they, rather than the speculators, should get the advantage of the higher average price.

This argument is not supported by either theory or experience. The much-reviled speculators are not the enemy of the farmer; they are essential to his best welfare. The risks of fluctuating farm prices must be borne by somebody; they have in fact been borne in modern times chiefly by the professional speculators. In general, the more competently the latter act in their own interest as speculators, the more they help the farmer. For speculators serve their own interest precisely in proportion to their ability to foresee future prices. But the more accurately they foresee future prices the less violent or extreme are the fluctuations in prices.

Even if farmers had to dump their whole crop of wheat on the market in a single month of the year, therefore, the price in that month would not necessarily be below the price at any other month (apart from an allowance for the costs of storage). For speculators, in the hope of making a profit, would do most of their buying at that time. They would keep on buying until the price rose to a point where they saw no further opportunity of future profit. They would sell whenever they thought there was a prospect of future loss. The result would be to stabilize the price of farm commodities the year round.

It is precisely because a professional class of speculators exists to take these risks that farmers and millers do not need to take them. The latter can protect themselves through the markets. Under normal conditions, therefore, when speculators are doing their job well, the profits of farmers and millers will depend chiefly on their skill and industry in farming or milling, and not on market fluctuations.

Actual experience shows that on the average the price of wheat and other nonperishable crops remains the same all year round except for an allowance for storage, interest and insurance charges. In fact, some careful investigations have shown that the average monthly rise after harvest time has not been quite sufficient to pay such storage charges, so that the speculators have actually subsidized the farmers. This, of course, was not their intention: it has simply been the result of a persistent tendency to overoptimism on the part of speculators. (This tendency seems to affect entrepreneurs in most competitive pursuits: as a class they are constantly, contrary to intention, subsidizing consumers. This is particularly true wherever the prospects of big speculative gains exist. Just as the subscribers to a lottery, considered as a unit, lose money because each is unjustifiably hopeful of drawing one of the few spectacular prizes, so it has been calculated that the total value of the labor and capital dumped into prospecting for gold or oil has exceeded the total value of the gold or oil extracted.)

The case is different, however, when the State steps in and either buys the farmers' crops itself or lends them the money to hold the crops off the market. This is sometimes done in the name of maintaining what is plausibly called an "ever-normal granary." But the history of prices and annual carryovers of crops shows that this function, as we have seen, is already being well performed by the privately organized free markets. When the government steps in, the ever-normal granary becomes in fact an ever-political granary. The farmer is encouraged, with the taxpayers' money, to withhold his crops excessively. Because they wish to make sure of retaining the farmer's vote, the politicians who initiate the policy, or the bureaucrats who carry it out, always place the so-called fair price for the farmer's product above the price that supply and demand conditions at the time justify. This leads to a falling off in buyers. The ever-normal granary therefore tends to become an ever-abnormal granary. Excessive stocks are held off the market. The effect of this is to secure a higher price temporarily than would otherwise exist, but to do so only by bringing about later on a much lower price than would otherwise have existed. For the artificial shortage built up this year by withholding part of a crop from the market means an artificial surplus the next year.

It would carry us too far afield to describe in detail what actually happened when this program was applied, for example, to American cotton.* We piled up an entire year's crop in storage. We destroyed the foreign market for our cotton. We stimulated enormously the growth of cotton in other countries. Though these results had been predicted by opponents of the restriction and loan policy, when they actually happened the bureaucrats responsible for the result merely replied that they would have happened anyway.

For the loan policy is usually accompanied by, or inevitably leads to, a policy of restricting production — i.e., a policy of scarcity. In nearly every effort to "stabilize" the price of a commodity, the interests of the producers have been put first. The real object is an immediate boost of prices. To make this possible, a proportional restriction of output is usually placed on each producer subject to the control. This has several immediately bad effects. Assuming that the control can be imposed on an international scale, it means that total world production is cut. The world's consumers are able to enjoy less of that product than they would have enjoyed without restriction. The world is just that much poorer. Because consum-

---

* The cotton program has been, however, an especially instructive one. As of August 1, 1956, the cotton carryover amounted to the record figure of 14,529,000 bales, more than a full year's normal production or consumption. To cope with this, the government changed its program. It decided to buy most of the crop from the growers and immediately offer it for resale at a discount. In order to sell American cotton again in the world market, it made a subsidy payment on cotton exports first of 6 cents a pound and, in 1961, of 8.5 cents a pound. This policy did succeed in reducing the raw-cotton carryover. But in addition to the losses it imposed on the taxpayers, it put American textiles at a serious competitive disadvantage with foreign textiles in both the domestic and foreign markets. The American government was subsidizing the foreign industry at the expense of the American industry. It is typical of government price-fixing schemes that they escape one undesired consequence only by plunging into another and usually worse one.[4]

ers are forced to pay higher prices than otherwise for that product, they have just that much less to spend on other products.

2

The restrictionists usually reply that this drop in output is what happens anyway under a market economy. But there is a fundamental difference, as we have seen in the preceding chapter. In a competitive market economy it is the high-cost producers, the *inefficient* producers, that are driven out by a fall in price. In the case of an agricultural commodity it is the least competent farmers, or those with the poorest equipment, or those working the poorest land, that are driven out. The most capable farmers on the best land do not have to restrict their production. On the contrary, if the fall in price has been symptomatic of a lower average cost of production, reflected through an increased supply, then the driving out of the marginal farmers on the marginal land enables the good farmers on the good land to *expand* their production. So there may be, in the long run, no reduction whatever in the output of that commodity. And the product is then produced and sold at a *permanently* lower price.

If that is the outcome, then the consumers of that commodity will be as well supplied with it as they were before. But, as a result of the lower price, they will have money left over, which they did not have before, to spend on other things. The consumers, therefore, will obviously be better off. But their increased spending in other directions will give increased employment in other lines, which will then absorb the former marginal farmers in occupations in which their efforts will be more lucrative and more efficient.

A uniform proportional restriction (to return to our government intervention scheme) means, on the one hand, that the efficient low-cost producers are not permitted to turn out all the output they can at a low price. It means, on the other hand, that the inefficient high-cost producers are artificially kept in business. This increases the average cost of producing the product. It is being produced less efficiently than otherwise. The inefficient marginal producer thus artificially kept in that line of production continues to tie up land, labor and capital that could much more profitably and efficiently be devoted to other uses.

There is no point in arguing that as a result of the restriction scheme at least the price of farm products has been raised and "the farmers have more purchasing power." They have got it only by taking just that much purchasing power away from the city buyer. (We have been over all this ground before in our analysis of parity prices.) To give farmers money for restricting production, or to give them the same amount of money for an artificially restricted production, is no different from forcing consumers or taxpayers to pay people for doing nothing at all. In each case the beneficiaries of such policies get "purchasing power." But in each case someone else loses an exactly equivalent amount. The net loss to the community is the loss of production, because people are supported for not producing. Because there is less for everybody, because there is less to go around, real wages and real incomes must decline either through a fall in their monetary amount or through higher living costs.

But if an attempt is made to keep up the price of an agricultural commodity and no artificial restriction of output is imposed, unsold surpluses of the overpriced commodity continue to pile up until the market for that product finally collapses to a far greater extent than if the control program had never been put into effect. Or producers outside the restriction program, stimulated by the artificial rise in price, expand their own production enormously. This is what happened in the British rubber-restriction and the American cotton-restriction programs. In either case the collapse of prices finally goes to catastrophic lengths that would never have been reached without the restriction scheme. The plan that started out so bravely to "stabilize" prices and conditions brings incomparably greater *in*stability than the free forces of the market could possibly have brought.

Yet new international commodity controls are constantly being proposed. *This* time, we are told, they are going to avoid all the old errors. This time prices are going to be fixed that are "fair" not only for producers but for consumers. Producing and consuming nations are going to agree on just what these fair prices are, because no one will be unreasonable. Fixed prices will necessarily involve "just" allotments and allocations for production and consumption as among nations, but only cynics will anticipate any unseemly international disputes regarding these. Finally, by the greatest miracle of all, this world of superinternational controls and coercions is also going to be a world of "free" international trade!

Just what the government planners mean by free trade in this connection I am not sure, but we can be sure of some of the things they do not mean. They do not mean the freedom of ordinary people to buy and sell, lend and borrow, at whatever prices or rates they like and wherever they find it most profitable to do so. They do not mean the freedom of the plain citizen to raise as much of a given crop as he wishes, to come and go at will, to settle where he pleases, to take his capital and other belongings with him. They mean, I suspect, the freedom of bureaucrats to settle these matters for him. And they tell him that if he docilely obeys the bureaucrats he will be rewarded by a rise in his living standards. But if the planners succeed in tying up the idea of international cooperation with the idea of increased State domination and control over economic life, the international controls of the future seem only too likely to follow the pattern of the past, in which case the plain man's living standards will decline with his liberties.

CHAPTER XVII

GOVERNMENT PRICE-FIXING

WE HAVE SEEN what some of the effects are of governmental efforts to fix the prices of commodities *above* the levels to which free markets would otherwise have carried them. Let us now look at some of the results of government attempts to hold the prices of commodities *below* their natural market levels.

The latter attempt is made in our day by nearly all governments in wartime. We shall not examine here the wisdom of wartime price-fixing. The whole economy, in total war, is necessarily dominated by the State, and the complications that would have to be considered would carry us too far beyond the main question with which this book is concerned.* But wartime price-fixing, wise or not, is in almost all countries continued for at least long periods after the war is over, when the original excuse for starting it has disappeared.

It is the wartime inflation that mainly causes the pressure for price-fixing. At the time of writing, when practically every country is inflating, though most of them are at peace, price controls are always hinted at, even when they are not imposed. Though they are always economically harmful, if not destructive, they have at least a political advantage from the standpoint of the officeholders.

---

* My own conclusion, however, is that, while some government priorities, allocations or rationing may be unavoidable, government price-fixing is likely to be *especially* harmful in total war. Whereas maximum price-fixing requires rationing to make it work, even temporarily, the converse is not true.

By implication they put the blame for higher prices on the greed and rapacity of businessmen, instead of on the inflationary monetary policies of the officeholders themselves.

Let us first see what happens when the government tries to keep the price of a single commodity, or a small group of commodities, below the price that would be set in a free competitive market.

When the government tries to fix maximum prices for only a few items, it usually chooses certain basic necessities, on the ground that it is most essential that the poor be able to obtain these at a "reasonable" cost. Let us say that the items chosen for this purpose are bread, milk and meat.

The argument for holding down the price of these goods will run something like this: If we leave beef (let us say) to the mercies of the free market, the price will be pushed up by competitive bidding so that only the rich will get it. People will get beef not in proportion to their need, but only in proportion to their purchasing power. If we keep the price down, everyone will get his fair share.

The first thing to be noticed about this argument is that if it is valid the policy adopted is inconsistent and timorous. For if purchasing power rather than need determines the distribution of beef at a market price of $2.25 cents a pound, it would also determine it, though perhaps to a slightly smaller degree, at, say, a legal "ceiling" price of $1.50 cents a pound. The purchasing-power-rather-than-need argument, in fact, holds as long as we charge anything for beef whatever. It would cease to apply only if beef were given away.

But schemes for maximum price-fixing usually begin as efforts to "keep the cost of living from rising." And so their sponsors unconsciously assume that there is something peculiarly "normal" or sacrosanct about the market price at the moment from which their control starts. That starting or previous price is regarded as "reasonable," and any price above that as "unreasonable," regardless of changes in the conditions of production or demand since that starting price was first established.

In discussing this subject, there is no point in assuming a price control that would fix prices exactly where a free market would place them in any case. That would be the same as having no price control at all. We must assume that the purchasing power in the hands of the public is greater than the supply of goods available, and that prices are being held down by the government *below* the levels to which a free market would put them.

Now we cannot hold the price of any commodity below its market level without in time bringing about two consequences. The first is to increase the demand for that commodity. Because the commodity is cheaper, people are both tempted to buy, and can afford to buy, more of it. The second consequence is to reduce the supply of that commodity. Because people buy more, the accumulated supply is more quickly taken from the shelves of merchants. But in addition to this, production of that commodity is discouraged. Profit margins are reduced or wiped out. The marginal producers are driven out of business. Even the most efficient producers may be called upon to turn out their product at a loss. This happened in World War II when slaughter houses were required by the Office of Price Administration to slaughter and process meat for less than the cost to them of cattle on the hoof and the labor of slaughter and processing.

If we did nothing else, therefore, the consequence of fixing a maximum price for a particular commodity would be to bring about a shortage of that commodity. But this is precisely the opposite of what the government regulators originally wanted to do. For it is the very commodities selected for maximum price-fixing that the regulators most want to keep in abundant supply. But when they limit the wages and the profits of those who make these commodities, without also limiting the wages and profits of those who make luxuries or semiluxuries, they discourage the production of the price-controlled necessities while they relatively stimulate the production of less essential goods.

Some of these consequences in time become apparent to the regulators, who then adopt various other devices and controls in an attempt to avert them. Among these devices are rationing, cost-control, subsidies, and universal price-fixing. Let us look at each of these in turn.

When it becomes obvious that a shortage of some commodity is developing as a result of a price fixed below the market, rich consumers are accused of taking "more than their fair share"; or, if it is a raw material that enters into manufacture, individual firms are accused of "hoarding" it. The government then adopts a set of rules concerning who shall have priority in buying that commodity, or to whom and in what quantities it shall be allocated, or how it shall be rationed. If a rationing system is adopted, it means that each consumer can have only a certain maximum supply, no matter how much he is willing to pay for more.

If a rationing system is adopted, in brief, it means that the government adopts a double price system, or a dual currency system, in which each consumer must have a certain number of coupons or "points" in addition to a given amount of ordinary money. In other words, the government tries to do through rationing part of the job that a free market would have done through prices. I say only part of the job, because rationing merely limits the demand without also stimulating the supply, as a higher price would have done.

The government may try to assure supply through extending its control over the costs of production of a commodity. To hold down the retail price of beef, for example, it may fix the wholesale price of beef, the slaughter-house price of beef, the price of live cattle, the price of feed, the wages of farmhands. To hold down the delivered price of milk, it may try to fix the wages of milk truck drivers, the price of containers, the farm price of milk, the price of feedstuffs. To fix the price of bread, it may fix the wages in bakeries, the price of flour, the profits of millers, the price of wheat, and so on.

But as the government extends this price-fixing backwards, it extends at the same time the consequences that originally drove it to this course. Assuming that it has the courage to fix these costs, and is able to enforce its decisions, then it merely, in turn, creates shortages of the various factors—labor, feedstuffs, wheat, or whatever—that enter into the production of the final commodities. Thus the government is driven to controls in ever-widening circles, and the final consequence will be the same as that of universal price-fixing.

The government may try to meet this difficulty through subsidies. It recognizes, for example, that when it keeps the price of milk or butter below the level of the market, or below the relative level at which it fixes other prices, a shortage may result because of lower wages or profit margins for the production of milk or butter as compared with other commodities. Therefore the government attempts to compensate for this by paying a subsidy to the milk and butter producers. Passing over the administrative difficulties involved in this, and assuming that the subsidy is just enough to assure the desired relative production of milk and butter, it is clear that, though the subsidy is paid to producers, those who are really being subsidized are the consumers. For the producers are on net balance getting no more for their milk and butter than if they had been allowed to charge the free market price in the first place; but the consumers are getting their milk and butter at a great deal below the free market price. They are being subsidized to the extent of the difference—that is, by the amount of subsidy paid ostensibly to the producers.

Now unless the subsidized commodity is also rationed, it is those with the most purchasing power that can buy most of it. This means that they are being subsidized more than those with less purchasing power. Who subsidizes the consumers will depend upon the incidence of taxation. But men in their role of taxpayers will be subsidizing themselves in their role of consumers. It becomes a little difficult to trace in this maze precisely who is subsidizing whom. What is forgotten is that subsidies are paid for by someone, and that no method has been discovered by which the community gets something for nothing.

3

Price-fixing may often appear for a short period to be successful. It can seem to work well for a while, particularly in wartime, when it is supported by patriotism and a sense of crisis. But the longer it is in effect the more its difficulties increase. When prices are arbitrarily held down by government compulsion, demand is *chronically* in excess of supply. We have seen that if the government attempts to prevent a shortage of a commodity by reducing also the prices of the labor, raw materials and other factors that go into its cost of production, it creates a shortage of these in turn. But not only will the government, if it pursues this course, find it necessary to extend price control more and more downwards, or "vertically"; it will find it no less necessary to extend price control "horizontally." If we ration one commodity, and the public cannot get enough of it, though it still has excess purchasing power, it will turn to some substitute. The rationing of each commodity as it grows scarce, in other words, must put more and more pressure on the unrationed commodities that remain. If we assume that the government is successful in its efforts to prevent black markets (or at least prevents them from developing on a sufficient scale to nullify its legal prices), continued price control must drive it to the rationing of more and more commodities. This rationing cannot stop with consumers. In World War II it did not stop with consumers. It was applied first of all, in fact, in the allocation of raw materials to producers.

The natural consequence of a thoroughgoing over-all price control which seeks to perpetuate a given historic price level, in brief, must ultimately be a completely regimented economy. Wages would have to be held down as rigidly as prices. Labor would have to be rationed as ruthlessly as raw materials. The end result would be that the government would not only tell each consumer precisely how much of each commodity he could have; it would tell each manufacturer precisely what quantity of each raw material he could have and what quantity of labor. Competitive bidding for workers could no more be tolerated than competitive bidding for materials. The result would be a petrified totalitarian economy, with every business firm and every worker at the mercy of the government, and with a final abandonment of all the traditional liberties we have known. For as Alexander Hamilton pointed out in the *Federalist Papers* nearly two centuries ago, "A power over a man's subsistence amounts to a power over his will."

4

These are the consequences of what might be described as "perfect," long-continued, and "nonpolitical" price control. As was so amply demonstrated in one country after another, particularly in Europe during and after World War II, some of the more fantastic errors of the bureaucrats were mitigated by the black market. In some countries the black market kept growing at the expense of the legally recognized fixed-price market until the former became, in effect, *the* market. By nominally keeping the price ceilings, however, the politicians in power tried to show that their hearts, if not their enforcement squads, were in the right place.

Because the black market, however, finally supplanted the legal price-ceiling market, it must not be supposed that no harm was done. The harm was both economic and moral. During the transition period the large, long-established firms, with a heavy capital investment and a great dependence upon the retention of public good-will, are forced to restrict or discontinue production. Their place is taken by fly-by-night concerns with little capital and little accumulated experience in production. These new firms are inefficient compared with those they displace; they turn out inferior and dishonest goods at much higher production costs than the older concerns would have required for continuing to turn out their former goods. A premium is put on dishonesty. The new firms owe their very existence or growth to the fact that they are willing to violate the law; their customers conspire with them; and as a natural consequence demoralization spreads into all business practices.

It is seldom, moreover, that any honest effort is made by the price-fixing authorities merely to preserve the level of prices existing when their efforts began. They declare that their intention is to "hold the line." Soon, however, under the guise of "correcting inequities" or "social injustices," they begin a discriminatory price-fixing which gives most to those groups that are politically powerful and least to other groups.

As political power today is most commonly measured by votes, the groups that the authorities most often attempt to favor are workers and farmers. At first it is contended that wages and living costs are not connected; that wages can easily be lifted without lifting prices. When it becomes obvious that wages can be raised only at the expense of profits, the bureaucrats begin to argue that profits were already too high anyway, and that lifting wages and holding prices will still permit a "fair profit." As there is no such thing as a uniform *rate* of profit, as profits differ with each concern, the result of this policy is to drive the least profitable concerns out of business altogether, and to discourage or stop the production of certain items. This means unemployment, a shrinkage in production and a decline in living standards.

5

What lies at the base of the whole effort to fix maximum prices? There is first of all a misunderstanding of what it is that has been causing prices to rise. The real cause is either a scarcity of goods or a surplus of money. Legal price ceilings cannot cure either. In fact, as we have just seen, they merely intensify the shortage of goods. What to do about the surplus of money will be discussed in a later chapter. But one of the errors that lie behind the drive for price-fixing is the chief subject of this book. Just as the endless plans for raising prices of favored commodities are the result of thinking of the interests only of the producers immediately concerned, and forgetting the interests of consumers, so the plans for holding down prices by legal edict are the result of thinking of the short-run interests of people only as consumers and forgetting their interests as producers. And the political support for such policies springs from a similar confusion in the public mind. People do not want to pay more for milk, butter, shoes, furniture, rent, theater tickets or diamonds. Whenever any of these items rises above its previous level the consumer becomes indignant, and feels that he is being rooked.

The only exception is the item he makes himself: here he understands and appreciates the reason for the rise. But he is always likely to regard his own business as in some way an exception. "Now my own business," he will say, "is peculiar, and the public does not understand it. Labor costs have gone up; raw material prices have gone up; this or that raw material is no longer being imported, and must be made at a higher cost at home. Moreover, the demand for the product has increased, and the business should be allowed to charge the prices necessary to encourage its expansion to supply this demand." And so on. Everyone as consumer buys a hundred different products; as producer he makes, usually, only one. He can see the inequity in holding down the price of *that*. And just as each manufacturer wants a higher price for his particular product, so each worker wants a higher wage or salary. Each can see as producer that price control is restricting production in his line. But nearly everyone refuses to generalize this observation, for it means that he will have to pay more for the products of *others*.

Each one of us, in brief, has a multiple economic personality. Each one of us is producer, taxpayer, consumer. The policies he advocates depend upon the particular aspect under which he thinks of himself at the moment. For he is sometimes Dr. Jekyll and sometimes Mr. Hyde. As a producer he wants inflation (thinking chiefly of his own services or product); as a consumer he wants price ceilings (thinking chiefly of what he has to pay for the products of others). As a consumer he may advocate or acquiesce in subsidies; as a taxpayer he will resent paying them. Each person is likely to think that he can so manage the political forces that he can benefit from a rise for his own product (while his raw material costs are legally held down) and at the same time benefit as a consumer from price control. But the overwhelming majority will be deceiving themselves. For not only must there be at least as much loss as gain from this political manipulation of prices; there must be a great deal more loss than gain, because price-fixing discourages and disrupts employment and production.

CHAPTER XVIII

WHAT RENT CONTROL DOES

GOVERNMENT CONTROL of the rents of houses and apartments is a special form of price control. Most of its consequences are substantially the same as those of price control in general, but a few call for special consideration.

Rent controls are sometimes imposed as a part of general price controls, but more often they are decreed by a special law. A frequent occasion is the beginning of a war. An army post is set up in a small town; rooming houses increase rents for rooms; owners of apartments and houses increase their rents. This leads to public indignation. Or houses in some towns may be actually destroyed by bombs, and the need for armaments or other supplies diverts materials and labor from the building trades.

Rent control is initially imposed on the argument that the supply of housing is not "elastic"—i.e., that a housing shortage cannot be immediately made up, no matter how high rents are allowed to rise. Therefore, it is contended, the government, by forbidding increases in rents, protects tenants from extortion and exploitation without doing any real harm to landlords and without discouraging new construction.

This argument is defective even on the assumption that the rent control will not long remain in effect. It overlooks an immediate consequence. If landlords are allowed to raise rents to reflect a monetary inflation and the true conditions of supply and demand, individual tenants will economize by taking less space. This will allow others to share the accommodations that are in short supply.

The same amount of housing will shelter more people, until the shortage is relieved.

Rent control, however, encourages wasteful use of space. It discriminates in favor of those who already occupy houses or apartments in a particular city or region at the expense of those who find themselves on the outside. Permitting rents to rise to the free market level allows all tenants or would-be tenants equal opportunity to bid for space. Under conditions of monetary inflation or real housing shortage, rents would rise just as surely if landlords were not allowed to set an asking price, but were allowed merely to accept the highest competitive bids of tenants.

The effects of rent control become worse the longer the rent control continues. New housing is not built because there is no incentive to build it. With the increase in building costs (commonly as a result of inflation), the old level of rents will not yield a profit. If, as often happens, the government finally recognizes this and exempts new housing from rent control, there is still not an incentive to as much new building as if older buildings were also free of rent control. Depending on the extent of money depreciation since old rents were legally frozen, rents for new housing might be ten or twenty times as high as rent in equivalent space in the old. (This actually happened in France after World War II, for example.) Under such conditions existing tenants in old buildings are indisposed to move, no matter how much their families grow or their existing accommodations deteriorate.

Because of low fixed rents in old buildings, the tenants already in them, and legally protected against rent increases, are encouraged to use space wastefully, whether or not their families have grown smaller. This concentrates the immediate pressure of new demand on the relatively few new buildings. It tends to force rents in them, at the beginning, to a higher level than they would have reached in a wholly free market.

Nevertheless, this will not correspondingly encourage the construction of new housing. Builders or owners of preexisting apartment houses, finding themselves with restricted profits or perhaps even losses on their old apartments, will have little or no capital to put into new construction. In addition, they, or those with capital from other sources, may fear that the government may at any time find an excuse for imposing rent controls even on the new buildings. And it often does.

The housing situation will deteriorate in other ways. Most important, unless the appropriate rent increases are allowed, landlords will not trouble to remodel apartments or make other improvements in them. In fact, where rent control is particularly unrealistic or oppressive, landlords will not even keep rented houses or apartments in tolerable repair. Not only will they have no economic incentive to do so; they may not even have the funds. The rent-control laws, among their other effects, create ill feeling between landlords who are forced to take minimum returns or even losses, and tenants who resent the landlord's failure to make adequate repairs.

A common next step of legislatures, acting under merely political pressures or confused economic ideas, is to take rent controls off "luxury" apartments while keeping them on low or middle-grade apartments. The argument is that the rich tenants can afford to pay higher rents, but the poor cannot.

The long-run effect of this discriminatory device, however, is the exact opposite of what its advocates intend. The builders and owners of luxury apartments are encouraged and rewarded; the builders and owners of the more needed low-rent housing are discouraged and penalized. The former are free to make as big a profit as the conditions of supply and demand warrant; the latter are left with no incentive (or even capital) to build more low-rent housing.

The result is a comparative encouragement to the repair and remodeling of luxury apartments, and a tendency for what new private building there is to be diverted to luxury apartments. But there is no incentive to build new low-income housing, or even to keep existing low-income housing in good repair. The accommodations for the low-income groups, therefore, will deteriorate in quality, and there will be no increase in quantity. Where the population is increasing, the deterioration and shortage in low-income housing will grow worse and worse. It may reach a point where many landlords not only cease to make any profit but are faced with mounting and compulsory losses. They may find that they cannot even give their property away. They may actually abandon their property and disappear, so they cannot be held liable for taxes. When owners cease supplying heat and other basic services, the tenants are compelled to abandon their apartments. Wider and wider neighborhoods are reduced to slums. In recent years, in New York City, it has become a common sight to see whole blocks of abandoned apartments, with windows broken, or boarded up to prevent further havoc by vandals. Arson becomes more frequent, and the owners are suspected.

A further effect is the erosion of city revenues, as the property-value base for such taxes continues to shrink. Cities go bankrupt, or cannot continue to supply basic services.

When these consequences are so clear that they become glaring, there is of course no acknowledgment on the part of the imposers of rent control that they have blundered. Instead, they denounce the capitalist system. They contend that private enterprise has "failed" again; that "private enterprise cannot do the job." Therefore, they argue, the State must step in and itself build low-rent housing.

This has been the almost universal result in every country that was involved in World War II or imposed rent control in an effort to offset monetary inflation.

So the government launches on a gigantic housing program—at the taxpayers' expense. The houses are rented at a rate that does not pay back costs of construction and operation. A typical arrangement is for the government to pay annual subsidies, either directly to the tenants in lower rents or to the builders or managers of the State housing. Whatever the nominal arrangement, the tenants in the buildings are being subsidized by the rest of the population. They are having part of their rent paid for them. They are being selected for favored treatment. The political possibilities of this favoritism are too clear to need stressing. A pressure group is built up that believes that the taxpayers owe it these subsidies as a matter of right. Another all but irreversible step is taken toward the total Welfare State.

A final irony of rent control is that the more unrealistic, Draconian, and unjust it is, the more fervid the political arguments for its continuance. If the legally fixed rents are on the average 95 percent as high as free market rents would be, and only minor injustice is being done to landlords, there is no strong political objection to taking off rent controls, because tenants will only have to pay increases averaging about 5 percent. But if the inflation of the currency has been so great, or the rent-control laws so repressive and unrealistic, that legally fixed rents are only 10 percent of what free market rents would be, and gross injustice is being done to owners and landlords, a great outcry will be raised about the dreadful evils of removing the controls and forcing tenants to pay an economic rent. The argument is made that it would be unspeakably cruel and unreasonable to ask the tenants to pay so sudden and huge an increase. Even the opponents of rent control are then disposed to concede that the removal of controls must be a very cautious, gradual, and prolonged process. Few of the opponents of rent control, indeed, have the political courage and economic insight under such conditions to ask even for this gradual decontrol. In sum, the more unrealistic and unjust the rent control is, the harder it is politically to get rid of it. In country after country, a ruinous rent control has been retained years after other forms of price control have been abandoned.

The political excuses offered for continuing rent control pass credibility. The law sometimes provides that the controls may be lifted when the "vacancy rate" is above a certain figure. The officials retaining the rent control keep triumphantly pointing out that the vacancy rate has not yet reached that figure. Of course not. The very fact that the legal rents are held so far below market rents artificially increases the demand for rental space at the same time as it discourages any increase in supply. So the more unreasonably low the rent ceilings are held, the more certain it is that the "scarcity" of rental houses or apartments will continue.

The injustice imposed on landlords is flagrant. They are, to repeat, forced to subsidize the rents paid by their tenants, often at the cost of great net losses to themselves. The subsidized tenants may frequently be richer than the landlord forced to assume part of what would otherwise be his market rent. The politicians ignore this. Men in other businesses, who support the imposition or retention of rent control because their hearts bleed for the tenants, do not go so far as to suggest that they themselves be asked to assume part of the tenant subsidy through taxation. The whole burden falls on the single small class of people wicked enough to have built or to own rental housing.

Few words carry stronger obloquy than *slumlord*. And what is a slumlord? He is not a man who owns expensive property in fashionable neighborhoods, but one who owns only rundown property in the slums, where the rents are lowest and where payment is most dilatory, erratic and undependable. It is not easy to imagine why (except for natural wickedness) a man who could afford to own decent rental housing would decide to become a slumlord instead.

When unreasonable price controls are placed on articles of immediate consumption, like bread, for example, the bakers can simply refuse to continue to bake and sell it. A shortage becomes immediately obvious, and the politicians are compelled to raise the ceilings or repeal them. But housing is very durable. It may take several years before tenants begin to feel the results of the discouragement to new building, and to ordinary maintenance and repair. It may take even longer before they realize that the scarcity and deterioration of housing is directly traceable to rent control. Meanwhile, as long as landlords are getting any net income whatever above their taxes and mortgage interest, they seem to have no alternative but to continue holding and renting their property. The politicians—remembering that tenants have more votes than landlords—cynically continue their rent control long after they have been forced to give up general price controls.

So we come back to our basic lesson. The pressure for rent control comes from those who consider only its imagined short-run benefits to one group in the population. But when we consider its *long-run* effects on *everybody*, including the tenants themselves, we recognize that rent control is not only increasingly futile, but increasingly destructive the more severe it is, and the longer it remains in effect.

CHAPTER XIX

MINIMUM WAGE LAWS

WE HAVE ALREADY seen some of the harmful results of arbitrary governmental efforts to raise the price of favored commodities. The same sort of harmful results follow efforts to raise wages through minimum wage laws. This ought not to be surprising, for a wage is, in fact, a price. It is unfortunate for clarity of economic thinking that the price of labor's services should have received an entirely different name from other prices. This has prevented most people from recognizing that the same principles govern both.

Thinking has become so emotional and so politically biased on the subject of wages that in most discussions of them the plainest principles are ignored. People who would be among the first to deny that prosperity could be brought about by artificially boosting prices, people who would be among the first to point out that minimum price laws might be most harmful to the very industries they were designed to help, will nevertheless advocate minimum wage laws, and denounce opponents of them, without misgivings.

Yet it ought to be clear that a minimum wage law is, at best, a limited weapon for combatting the evil of low wages, and that the possible good to be achieved by such a law can exceed the possible harm only in proportion as its aims are modest. The more ambitious such a law is, the larger the number of workers it attempts to cover, and the more it attempts to raise their wages, the more certain are its harmful effects to exceed any possible good effects.

The first thing that happens, for example, when a law is passed that no one shall be paid less than $106 for a forty-hour week is that no one who is not worth $106 a week to an employer will be employed at all. You cannot make a man worth a given amount by making it illegal for anyone to offer him anything less. You merely deprive him of the right to earn the amount that his abilities and situation would permit him to earn, while you deprive the community even of the moderate services that he is capable of rendering. In brief, for a low wage you substitute unemployment. You do harm all around, with no comparable compensation.

The only exception to this occurs when a group of workers is receiving a wage actually below its market worth. This is likely to happen only in rare and special circumstances or localities where competitive forces do not operate freely or adequately; but nearly all these special cases could be remedied just as effectively, more flexibly and with far less potential harm, by unionization.

It may be thought that if the law forces the payment of a higher wage in a given industry, that industry can then charge higher prices for its product, so that the burden of paying the higher wage is merely shifted to consumers. Such shifts, however, are not easily made, nor are the consequences of artificial wage-raising so easily escaped. A higher price for the product may not be possible: it may merely drive consumers to the equivalent imported products or to some substitute. Or, if consumers continue to buy the product of the industry in which wages have been raised, the higher price will cause them to buy less of it. While some workers in the industry may be benefited from the higher wage, therefore, others will be thrown out of employment altogether. On the other hand, if the price of the product is not raised, marginal producers in the industry will be driven out of business; so that reduced production and consequent unemployment will merely be brought about in another way.

When such consequences are pointed out, there are those who reply: "Very well; if it is true that the X industry cannot exist except by paying starvation wages, then it will be just as well if the minimum wage puts it out of existence altogether." But this brave pronouncement overlooks the realities. It overlooks, first of all, that consumers will suffer the loss of that product. It forgets, in the second place, that it is merely condemning the people who worked in that industry to unemployment. And it ignores, finally, that bad as were the wages paid in the X industry, they were the best among all the alternatives that seemed open to the workers in that industry; otherwise the workers would have gone into another. If, therefore, the X industry is driven out of existence by a minimum wage law, then the workers previously employed in that industry will be forced to turn to alternative courses that seemed less attractive to them in the first place. Their competition for jobs will drive down the pay offered even in these alternative occupations. There is no escape from the conclusion that the minimum wage will increase unemployment.

2

A nice problem, moreover, will be raised by the relief program designed to take care of the unemployment caused by the minimum wage law. By a minimum wage of, say, $2.65 an hour, we have forbidden anyone to work forty hours in a week for less than $106.[5] Suppose, now, we offer only $70 a week on relief. This means that we have forbidden a man to be usefully employed at, say, $90 a week, in order that we may support him at $70 a week in idleness. We have deprived society of the value of his services. We have deprived the man of the independence and self-respect that come from self-support, even at a low level, and from performing wanted work, at the same time as we have lowered what the man could have received by his own efforts.

These consequences follow as long as the weekly relief payment is a penny less than $106. Yet the higher we make the relief payment, the worse we make the situation in other respects. If we offer $106 for relief, then we offer many men just as much for not working as for working. Moreover, whatever the sum we offer for relief, we create a situation in which everyone is working only for the *difference* between his wages and the amount of the relief. If the relief is $106 a week, for example, workers offered a wage of $2.75 an hour, or $110 a week, are in fact, as they see it, being asked to work for only $4 a week—for they can get the rest without doing anything.

It may be thought that we can escape these consequences by offering "work relief" instead of "home relief"; but we merely change the nature of the consequences. Work relief means that we are paying the beneficiaries more than the open market would pay them for their efforts. Only part of their relief-wage is for their efforts, therefore, while the rest is a disguised dole.

It remains to be pointed out that government make-work is necessarily inefficient and of questionable utility. The government has to invent projects that will employ the least skilled. It cannot start teaching people carpentry, masonry, and the like, for fear of competing with established skills and arousing the antagonism of existing unions. I am not recommending it, but it probably would be less harmful all around if the government in the first place frankly subsidized the wages of submarginal workers at the work they were already doing. Yet this would create political headaches of its own.

We need not pursue this point further, as it would carry us into problems not immediately relevant. But the difficulties and consequences of relief must be kept in mind when we consider the adoption of minimum wage laws or an increase in minimums already fixed.[*]

---

[*] In 1938, when the average hourly wage paid in all manufacturing in the United States was about 63 cents an hour, Congress set a legal minimum of only 25 cents. In 1945, when the average factory wage had risen to $1.02 an hour, Congress raised the legal minimum to 40 cents. In 1949, when the average factory wage had risen to $1.40 an hour, Congress raised the minimum again to 75 cents. In 1955, when the average had risen to $1.88, Congress boosted the minimum to $1. In 1961, with the average factory wage at about $2.30 an hour, the minimum was raised to $1.15 in 1961 and to $1.25 for 1963. To shorten the account, the minimum wage was raised to $1.40 in 1967, to $1.60 in 1968, to $2.00 in 1974, to $2.10 in 1975, and to $2.30 in 1976 (when the average wage in all private nonagricultural work was $4.87) Then in 1977, when the actual average hourly wage in nonagricultural work was $5.26, the minimum wage was raised to $2.65 an hour, with provision made for notching it up still further

Before we finish with the topic I should perhaps mention another argument sometimes put forward for fixing a minimum wage rate by statute. This is that in an industry in which one big company enjoys a monopoly, it need not fear competition and can offer below-market wages. This is a highly improbable situation. Such a "monopoly" company must offer high wages when it is formed, in order to attract labor from other industries. Thereafter it could theoretically fail to increase wage rates as much as other industries, and so pay "substandard" wages for that particular specialized skill. But this would be likely to happen only if that industry (or company) was sick or shrinking; if it were prosperous or expanding, it would have to continue to offer high wages to increase its labor force.

We know as a matter of experience that it is the big companies — those most often accused of being monopolies — that pay the highest wages and offer the most attractive working conditions. It is commonly the small marginal firms, perhaps suffering from excessive competition, that offer the lowest wages. But all employers must pay enough to hold workers or to attract them from each other.

3

All this is not to argue that there is no way of raising wages. It is merely to point out that the apparently easy method of raising them by government fiat is the wrong way and the worst way.

This is perhaps as good a place as any to point out that what distinguishes many reformers from those who cannot accept their proposals is not their greater philanthropy, but their greater impa-

---

in each of the next three years. Thus, as the prevailing hourly wage goes higher, the minimum wage advocates decide that the legal minimum must be raised at least correspondingly. Though the legislation follows the rise of the prevailing market wage rate, the myth continues to be built up that it is the minimum wage legislation that has raised the market wage.[6]

tience. The question is not whether we wish to see everybody as well off as possible. Among men of good will such an aim can be taken for granted. The real question concerns the proper means of achieving it. And in trying to answer this we must never lose sight of a few elementary truisms. We cannot distribute more wealth than is created. We cannot in the long run pay labor as a whole more than it produces.

The best way to raise wages, therefore, is to raise marginal labor productivity. This can be done by many methods: by an increase in capital accumulation—i.e., by an increase in the machines with which the workers are aided; by new inventions and improvements; by more efficient management on the part of employers; by more industriousness and efficiency on the part of workers; by better education and training. The more the individual worker produces, the more he increases the wealth of the whole community. The more he produces, the more his services are worth to consumers, and hence to employers. And the more he is worth to employers, the more he will be paid. Real wages come out of production, not out of government decrees.

So government policy should be directed, not to imposing more burdensome requirements on employers, but to following policies that encourage profits, that encourage employers to expand, to invest in newer and better machines to increase the productivity of workers—in brief, to encourage capital accumulation, instead of discouraging it—and to increase both employment and wage rates.

CHAPTER XX

DO UNIONS REALLY RAISE WAGES?

THE BELIEF THAT labor unions can substantially raise real wages over the long run and for the whole working population is one of the great delusions of the present age. This delusion is mainly the result of failure to recognize that wages are basically determined by labor productivity. It is for this reason, for example, that wages in the United States were incomparably higher than wages in England and Germany all during the decades when the "labor movement" in the latter two countries was far more advanced.

In spite of the overwhelming evidence that labor productivity is the fundamental determinant of wages, the conclusion is usually forgotten or derided by labor union leaders and by that large group of economic writers who seek a reputation as "liberals" by parroting them. But this conclusion does not rest on the assumption, as they suppose, that employers are uniformly kind and generous men eager to do what is right. It rests on the very different assumption that the individual employer is eager to increase his own profits to the maximum. If people are willing to work for less than they are really worth to him, why should he not take the fullest advantage of this? Why should he not prefer, for example, to make $1 a week out of a workman rather than see some other employer make $2 a week out of him? And as long as this situation exists, there will be a tendency for employers to bid workers up to their full economic worth.

All this does not mean that unions can serve no useful or legitimate function. The central function they can serve is to improve local working conditions and to assure that all of their members get the true market value of their services.

For the competition of workers for jobs, and of employers for workers, does not work perfectly. Neither individual workers nor individual employers are likely to be fully informed concerning the conditions of the labor market. An individual worker may not know the true market value of his services to an employer. And he may be in a weak bargaining position. Mistakes of judgment are far more costly to him than to an employer. If an employer mistakenly refuses to hire a man from whose services he might have profited, he merely loses the net profit he might have made from employing that one man; and he may employ a hundred or a thousand men. But if a worker mistakenly refuses a job in the belief that he can easily get another that will pay him more, the error may cost him dear. His whole means of livelihood is involved. Not only may he fail to find promptly another job offering more; he may fail for a time to find another job offering remotely as much. And time may be the essence of his problem, because he and his family must eat. So he may be tempted to take a wage that he believes to be below his "real worth" rather than face these risks. When an employer's workers deal with him as a body, however, and set a known "standard wage" for a given class of work, they may help to equalize bargaining power and the risks involved in mistakes.

But it is easy, as experience has proved, for unions, particularly with the help of one-sided labor legislation which puts compulsions solely on employers, to go beyond their legitimate functions, to act irresponsibly, and to embrace short-sighted and antisocial policies. They do this, for example, whenever they seek to fix the wages of their members above their real market worth. Such an attempt always brings about unemployment. The arrangement can be made to stick, in fact, only by some form of intimidation or coercion.

One device consists in restricting the membership of the union on some other basis than that of proved competence or skill. This restriction may take many forms: it may consist in charging new workers excessive initiation fees; in arbitrary membership qualifications; in discrimination, open or concealed, on grounds of religion, race or sex; in some absolute limitation on the number of members, or in exclusion, by force if necessary, not only of the products of nonunion labor, but of the products even of affiliated unions in other states or cities.

The most obvious case in which intimidation and force are used to put or keep the wages of a particular union above the real market worth of its members' services is that of a strike. A peaceful strike is possible. To the extent that it remains peaceful, it is a legitimate labor weapon, even though it is one that should be used rarely and as a last resort. If his workers as a body withhold their labor, they may bring a stubborn employer, who has been underpaying them, to his senses. He may find that he is unable to replace these workers with workers equally good who are willing to accept the wage that the former have now rejected. But the moment workers have to use intimidation or violence to enforce their demands—the moment they use mass picketing to prevent any of the old workers from continuing at their jobs, or to prevent the employer from hiring new permanent workers to take their places—their case becomes suspect. For the pickets are really being used, not primarily against the employer, but against other workers. These other workers are willing to take the jobs that the old employees have vacated, and at the wages that the old employees now reject. The fact proves that the other alternatives open to the new workers are not as good as those that the old employees have refused. If, therefore, the old employees succeed by force in preventing new workers from taking the place, they prevent these new workers from choosing the best alternative open to them, and force them to take something worse. The strikers are therefore insisting on a position of privilege, and are using force to maintain this privileged position against other workers.

If the foregoing analysis is correct, the indiscriminate hatred of the "strikebreaker" is not justified. If the strikebreakers consist merely of professional thugs who themselves threaten violence, or who cannot in fact do the work, or if they are being paid a temporarily higher rate solely for the purpose of making a pretense of carrying on until the old workers are frightened back to work at the old rates, the hatred may be warranted. But if they are in fact merely men and women who are looking for permanent jobs and willing to accept them at the old rate, then they are workers who would be shoved into worse jobs than these in order to enable the striking workers to enjoy better ones. And this superior position for the old employees could continue to be maintained, in fact, only by the ever-present threat of force.

2

Emotional economics has given birth to theories that calm examination cannot justify. One of these is the idea that labor is being "underpaid"*generally*. This would be analogous to the notion that in a free market prices in general are chronically too low. Another curious but persistent notion is that the interests of a nation's workers are identical with each other, and that an increase in wages for one union in some obscure way helps all other workers. Not only is there no truth in this idea; the truth is that, if a particular union by coercion is able to enforce for its own members a wage substantially above the real market worth of their services, it will hurt all other workers as it hurts other members of the community.

In order to see more clearly how this occurs, let us imagine a community in which the facts are enormously simplified arithmetically. Suppose the community consisted of just half a dozen groups of workers, and that these groups were originally equal to each other in their total wages and the market value of their product.

Let us say that these six groups of workers consist of (1) farm hands, (2) retail store workers, (3) workers in the clothing trades, (4) coal miners, (5) building workers, and (6) railway employees. Their wage rates, determined without any element of coercion, are not necessarily equal; but whatever they are, let us assign to each of them an original index number of 100 as a base. Now let us suppose that each group forms a national union and is able to enforce its demands in proportion not merely to its economic productivity but to its political power and strategic position. Suppose the result is that the farm hands are unable to raise their wages at all, that the retail store workers are able to get an increase of 10 percent, the clothing workers of 20 percent, the coal miners of 30 percent, the building trades of 40 percent, and the railroad employees of 50 percent.

On the assumptions we have made, this will mean that there has been an *average* increase in wages of 25 percent. Now suppose, again for the sake of arithmetical simplicity, that the price of the product that each group of workers makes rises by the same percentage as the increase in that group's wages. (For several reasons, including the fact that labor costs do not represent all costs, the price will not quite do that—certainly not in any short period. But the figures will nonetheless serve to illustrate the basic principle involved.)

We shall then have a situation in which the cost of living has risen by an average of 25 percent. The farm hands, though they have had no reduction in their money wages, will be considerably worse off in terms of what they can buy. The retail store workers, even though they have got an increase in money wages of 10 percent, will be worse off than before the race began. Even the workers in the clothing trades, with a money-wage increase of 20 percent, will be at a disadvantage compared with their previous position. The coal miners, with a money-wage increase of 30 percent, will have made in purchasing power only a slight gain. The building and railroad workers will of course have made a gain, but one much smaller in actuality than in appearance.

But even such calculations rest on the assumption that the forced increase in wages has brought about no unemployment. This is likely to be true only if the increase in wages has been accompanied by an equivalent increase in money and bank credit; and even then it is improbable that such distortions in wage rates can be brought about without creating areas of unemployment, particularly in the trades in which wages have advanced the most. If this corresponding monetary inflation does not occur, the forced wage advances will bring about widespread unemployment.

The unemployment need not necessarily be greatest, in percentage terms, among the unions whose wages have been advanced the most; for unemployment will be shifted and distributed in relation to the relative elasticity of the demand for different kinds of labor and in relation to the "joint" nature of the demand for many kinds of labor. Yet when all these allowances have been made, even the groups whose wages have been advanced the most will probably be found, when their unemployed are averaged with their employed members, to be worse off than before. And in terms of *welfare*, of course, the loss suffered will be much greater than the loss in merely arithmetical terms, because the psychological losses of those who are unemployed will greatly outweigh the psychological gains of those with a slightly higher income in terms of purchasing power.

Nor can the situation be rectified by providing unemployment relief. Such relief, in the first place, is paid for in large part, directly or indirectly, out of the wages of those who work. It therefore reduces these wages. "Adequate" relief payments, moreover, as we have already seen, *create* unemployment. They do so in several ways. When strong labor unions in the past made it their function to provide for their own unemployed members, they thought twice before demanding a wage that would cause heavy unemployment. But where there is a relief system under which the general taxpayer is forced to provide for the unemployment caused by excessive wage rates, this restraint on excessive union demands is removed. Moreover, as we have already noted, "adequate" relief will cause some men not to seek work at all, and will cause others to consider that they are in effect being asked to work not for the wage offered, but only for the *difference* between that wage and the relief payment. And heavy unemployment means that fewer goods are produced, that the nation is poorer, and that there is less for everybody.

The apostles of salvation by unionism sometimes attempt another answer to the problem I have just presented. It may be true, they will admit, that the members of strong unions today exploit among others, the nonunionized workers; but the remedy is simple: unionize everybody. The remedy, however, is not quite that simple. In the first place, in spite of the enormous legal and political encouragements (one might in some cases say compulsions) to unionization under the Wagner-Taft-Hartley Act and other laws, it is not an accident that only about a fourth of this nation's gainfully employed workers are unionized.[7] The conditions propitious to unionization are much more special than generally recognized. But even if universal unionization could be achieved, the unions could not possibly be equally powerful, any more than they are today. Some groups of workers are in a far better strategic position than others, either because of greater numbers, of the more essential nature of the product they make, of the greater dependence on their industry of other industries, or of their greater ability to use coercive methods. But suppose this were not so? Suppose, in spite of the self-contradictoriness of the assumption, that all workers by coercive methods could raise their money wages by an equal percentage? Nobody would be any better off in the long run, than if wages had not been raised at all.

3

This leads us to the heart of the question. It is usually assumed that an increase in wages is gained at the expense of the profits of employers. This may of course happen for short periods or in special circumstances. If wages are forced up in a particular firm, in such competition with others that it cannot raise its prices, the increase will come out of its profits. This is less likely to happen if the wage increase takes place throughout a whole industry. If the industry does not face foreign competition it may be able to increase its prices and pass the wage increase along to consumers. As these are likely to consist for the most part of workers, they will simply have their real wages reduced by having to pay more for a particular product. It is true that as a result of the increased prices, sales of that industry's products may fall off, so that volume of profits in the industry will be reduced; but employment and total payrolls in the industry are likely to be reduced by a corresponding amount.

It is possible, no doubt, to conceive of a case in which the profits in a whole industry are reduced without any corresponding reduction in employment—a case, in other words, in which an increase in wage rates means a corresponding increase in payrolls, and in which the whole cost comes out of the industry's profits without throwing any firm out of business. Such a result is not likely, but it is conceivable.

Suppose we take an industry like that of the railroads, for example, which cannot always pass increased wages along to the public in the form of higher rates, because government regulation will not permit it.

It is at least possible for unions to make their gains in the short run at the expense of employers and investors. The investors once had liquid funds. But they have put them, say, into the railroad business. They have turned them into rails and roadbeds, freight cars and locomotives. Once their capital might have been turned into any of a thousand forms, but today it is *trapped*, so to speak, in one specific form. The railway unions may force them to accept smaller returns on this capital already invested. It will pay the investors to continue running the railroad if they can earn anything at all above operating expenses, even if it is only one-tenth of one percent on their investment.

But there is an inevitable corollary of this. If the money that they have invested in railroads now yields less than money they can invest in other lines, the investors will not put a cent more into railroads. They may replace a few of the things that wear out first, to protect the small yield on their remaining capital; but in the long run they will not even bother to replace items that fall into obsolescence or decay. If capital invested at home pays them less than that invested abroad, they will invest abroad. If they cannot find sufficient return anywhere to compensate them for their risk, they will cease to invest at all.

Thus the exploitation of capital by labor can at best he merely temporary. It will quickly come to an end. It will come to an end, actually, not so much in the way indicated in our hypothetical illustration, as by the forcing of marginal firms out of business entirely, the growth of unemployment, and the forced readjustment of wages and profits to the point where the prospect of normal (or abnormal) profits leads to a resumption of employment and production. But in the meanwhile, as a result of the exploitation, unemployment and reduced production will have made everybody poorer. Even though labor for a time will have a greater *relative* share of the national income, the national income will fall absolutely; so that labor's relative gains in these short periods may mean a Pyrrhic victory: they may mean that labor, too, is getting a lower total amount in terms of real purchasing power.

4

Thus we are driven to the conclusion that unions, though they may for a time be able to secure an increase in money wages for their members, partly at the expense of employers and more at the expense of nonunionized workers, *cannot, in the long-run and for the whole body of workers, increase real wages at all.*

The belief that they do so rests on a series of delusions. One of these is the fallacy of *post hoc ergo propter hoc*, which sees the enormous rise in wages in the last half century, due principally to the growth of capital investment and to scientific and technological advance, and ascribes it to the unions because the unions were also growing during this period. But the error most responsible for the delusion is that of considering merely what a rise of wages brought about by union demands means in the short run for the particular workers who retain their jobs, while failing to trace the effects of this advance on employment, production and the living costs of all workers, including those who forced the increase.

One may go further than this conclusion, and raise the question whether unions have not, in the long run and for the whole body of workers, actually prevented real wages from rising to the extent to which they otherwise might have risen. They have certainly been a force working to hold down or to reduce wages if their effect, on net balance, has been to reduce labor productivity; and we may ask whether it has not been so.

With regard to productivity there is something to be said for union policies, it is true, on the credit side. In some trades they have insisted on standards to increase the level of skill and competence. And in their early history they did much to protect the health of their members. Where labor was plentiful, individual employers often stood to make short-run gains by speeding up workers and working them long hours in spite of ultimate ill effects upon their health, because they could easily be replaced with others. And sometimes ignorant or shortsighted employers might even reduce their own profits by overworking their employees. In all these cases the unions, by demanding decent standards, often increased the health and broader welfare of their members at the same time as they increased their real wages.

But in recent years, as their power has grown, and as much misdirected public sympathy has led to a tolerance or endorsement of antisocial practices, unions have gone beyond their legitimate goals. It was a gain, not only to health and welfare, but even in the long run to production, to reduce a seventy-hour week to a sixty-hour week. It was a gain to health and leisure to reduce a sixty-hour week to a forty-eight-hour week. It was a gain to leisure, but not necessarily to production and income, to reduce a forty-eight-hour week to a forty-four-hour week. The value to health and leisure of reducing the working week to forty hours is much less, the reduction in output and income more clear. But the unions now talk about, and sometimes enforce, thirty-five and thirty-hour weeks, and deny that these can or need reduce output or income.

But it is not only in reducing scheduled working hours that union policy has worked against productivity. That, in fact, is one of the least harmful ways in which it has done so; for the compensating gain, at least, has been clear. But many unions have insisted on rigid subdivisions of labor which have raised production costs and led to expensive and ridiculous "jurisdictional" disputes. They have opposed payment on the basis of output or efficiency, and insisted on the same hourly rates for all their members regardless of differences in productivity. They have insisted on promotion for seniority rather than for merit. They have initiated deliberate slowdowns under the pretense of fighting "speed-ups." They have denounced, insisted upon the dismissal of, and sometimes cruelly beaten, men who turned out more work than their fellows. They have opposed the introduction or improvement of machinery. They have insisted that if any of their members have been laid off because of the installation of more efficient or more laborsaving machinery, the laid-off workers receive "guaranteed incomes" indefinitely. They have insisted on make-work rules to require more people or more time to perform a given task. They have even insisted, with the threat of ruining employers, on the hiring of people who are not needed at all.

Most of these policies have been followed under the assumption that there is just a fixed amount of work to be done, a definite "job fund" which has to be spread over as many people and hours as possible so as not to use it up too soon. This assumption is utterly false. There is actually no limit to the amount of work to be done. Work creates work. What A produces constitutes the demand for what B produces.

But because this false assumption exists, and because the policies of unions are based on it, their net effect has been to reduce productivity below what it would otherwise have been. Their net effect, therefore, in the long run and for all groups of workers, has been to *reduce* real wages—that is, wages in terms of the goods they will buy—below the level to which they would otherwise have risen. The real cause for the tremendous increase in real wages in the last century has been, to repeat, the accumulation of capital and the enormous technological advance made possible by it.

But this process is not automatic. As a result not only of bad union but of bad governmental policies, it has, in fact, in the last decade, come to a halt. If we look only at the average of gross weekly earnings of private nonagricultural workers in terms of paper dollars, it is true that they have risen from $107.73 in 1968 to $189.36 in August 1977. But when the Bureau of Labor Statistics allows for inflation, when it translates these earnings into 1967 dollars, to take account of the increase in consumer prices, it finds that real weekly earnings actually fell from $103.39 in 1968 to $103.36 in August 1977.[8]

This halt in the rise of real wages has not been a consequence inherent in the nature of unions. It has been the result of short-sighted union and government policies. There is still time to change both of them.

CHAPTER XXI

"ENOUGH TO BUY BACK THE PRODUCT"

AMATEUR WRITERS on economics are always asking for "just" prices and "just" wages. These nebulous conceptions of economic justice come down to us from medieval times. The classical economists worked out instead, a different concept—the concept of *functional* prices and *functional* wages. Functional prices are those that encourage the largest volume of production and the largest volume of sales. Functional wages are those that tend to bring about the highest volume of employment and the largest real payrolls.

The concept of functional wages has been taken over, in a perverted form, by the Marxists and their unconscious disciples, the purchasing-power school. Both of these groups leave to cruder minds the question whether existing wages are "fair." The real question, they insist, is whether or not they will *work*. And the only wages that will work, they tell us, the only wages that will prevent an imminent economic crash, are wages that will enable labor "to buy back the product it creates." The Marxist and purchasing-power schools attribute every depression of the past to a preceding failure to pay such wages. And at no matter what moment they speak, they are sure that wages are still not high enough to buy back the product.

The doctrine has proved particularly effective in the hands of union leaders. Despairing of their ability to arouse the altruistic interest of the public or to persuade employers (wicked by definition) ever to be "fair," they have seized upon an argument calculated to appeal to the public's selfish motives, and frighten it into forcing employers to grant union demands.

How are we to know, however, precisely when labor does have "enough to buy back the product"? Or when it has more than enough? How are we to determine just what the right sum is? As the champions of the doctrine do not seem to have made any real effort to answer such questions, we are obliged to try to find the answers for ourselves.

Some sponsors of the theory seem to imply that the workers in each industry should receive enough to buy back the particular product they make. But they surely cannot mean that the makers of cheap dresses should get enough to buy back cheap dresses and the makers of mink coats enough to buy back mink coats; or that the men in the Ford plant should receive enough to buy Fords and the men in the Cadillac plant enough to buy Cadillacs.

It is instructive to recall, however, that the unions in the automobile industry, in the 1940s, when most of their members were already in the upper third of the country's income receivers, and when their weekly wage, according to government figures, was already 20 percent higher than the average wage paid in factories and nearly twice as great as the average paid in retail trade, were demanding a 30 percent increase so that they might, according to one of their spokesmen, "bolster our fast-shrinking ability to absorb the goods which we have the capacity to produce."

What, then, of the average factory worker and the average retail worker? If, under such circumstances, the automobile workers needed a 30 percent increase to keep the economy from collapsing, would a mere 30 percent have been enough for the others? Or would they have required increases of 55 to 160 percent to give them as much per capita purchasing power as the automobile workers? For let us remember that then as now enormous differences existed between the average wage levels of different industries. In 1976, workers in retail trade averaged weekly earnings of only $113.96, while workers in all manufacturing averaged $207.60 and those in contract construction $284.93

(We may be sure, if the history of wage bargaining even *within individual unions* is any guide, that the automobile workers, if this last proposal had been made, would have insisted on the mainte-nance of their existing differentials; for the passion for economic equality, among union members as among the rest of us, is, with the exception of a few rare philanthropists and saints, a passion for getting as much as those above us in the economic scale already get rather than a passion for giving those below us as much as we ourselves already get. But it is with the logic and soundness of a particular economic theory, rather than with these distressing weaknesses of human nature, that we are at present concerned.)

2

The argument that labor should receive enough to buy back the product is merely a special form of the general "purchasing-power" argument. The workers' wages, it is correctly enough contended, are the workers' purchasing power. But it is just as true that everyone's income—the grocer's, the landlord's, the employer's—is his purchasing power for buying what others have to sell. And one of the most important things for which others have to find purchasers is their labor services.

All this, moreover, has its reverse side. *In an exchange economy everybody's money income is somebody else's cost.* Every increase in hourly wages, unless or until compensated by an equal increase in hourly productivity, is an increase in costs of production. An increase in costs of production, where the government controls prices and forbids any price increase, takes the profit from marginal producers, forces them out of business, and means a shrinkage in production and a growth in unemployment. Even where a price increase is possible, the higher price discourages buyers, shrinks the market, and also leads to unemployment. If a 30 percent increase in hourly wages all around the circle forces a 30 percent increase in prices, labor can buy no more of the product than it could at the beginning; and the merry-go-round must start all over again.

No doubt many will be inclined to dispute the contention that a 30 percent increase in wages can force as great a percentage increase in prices. It is true that this result can follow only in the long run and only if monetary and credit policy permit it. If money and credit are so inelastic that they do not increase when wages are forced up (and if we assume that the higher wages are not justified by existing labor productivity in dollar terms), then the chief effect of forcing up wage rates will be to force unemployment.

And it is probable, in that case, that total payrolls, both in dollar amount and in real purchasing power, will be lower than before. For a drop in employment (brought about by union policy and not as a transitional result of technological advance) necessarily means that fewer goods are being produced for everyone. And it is unlikely that labor will compensate for the absolute drop in production by getting a larger relative share of the production that is left. For Paul H. Douglas in America and A. C. Pigou in England, the first from analyzing a great mass of statistics, the second by almost purely deductive methods, arrived independently at the conclusion that the elasticity of the demand for labor is somewhere between 3 and 4. This means, in less technical language, that "a 1 percent reduction in the real rate of wage is likely to expand the aggregate demand for labor by not less than 3 percent."[*] Or, to put the matter the other way, "If wages are pushed up above the point of marginal productivity, the decrease in employment would normally be from three to four times as great as the increase in hourly rates"[†] so that the total incomes of the workers would be reduced correspondingly.

---

[*] A. C. Pigou, *The Theory of Unemployment* (1933), p. 96.
[†] Paul H. Douglas, *The Theory of Wages* (1934), p. 501.

Even if these figures are taken to represent only the elasticity of the demand for labor revealed in a given period of the past and not necessarily to forecast that of the future, they deserve the most serious consideration.

3

But now let us suppose that the increase in wage rates is accompanied or followed by a sufficient increase in money and credit to allow it to take place without creating serious unemployment. If we assume that the previous relationship between wages and prices was itself a "normal" long-run relationship, then it is altogether probable that a forced increase of, say, 30 percent in wage rates will ultimately lead to an increase in prices of approximately the same percentage.

The belief that the price increase would be substantially less than that rests on two main fallacies. The first is that of looking only at the direct labor costs of a particular firm or industry and assuming these to represent all the labor costs involved. But this is the elementary error of mistaking a part for the whole. Each "industry" represents not only just one section of the productive process considered "horizontally," but just one section of that process considered "vertically." Thus the direct labor cost of making automobiles in the automobile factories themselves may be less than a third, say, of the total costs; and this may lead the incautious to conclude that a 30 percent increase in wages would lead to only a 10 percent increase, or less, in automobile prices. But this would be to overlook the indirect wage costs in the raw materials and purchased parts, in transportation charges, in new factories or new machine tools, or in the dealers' mark-up.

Government estimates show that in the fifteen-year period from 1929 to 1943, inclusive, wages and salaries in the United States averaged 69 percent of the national income. In the five-year period 1956–1960 they also averaged 69 percent of the national income! In the five-year period 1972–1976 wages and salaries averaged 66 percent of national income, and when supplements are added, total compensation of employees averaged 76 percent of national income.[9] These wages and salaries, of course, had to be paid out of the national product. While there would have to be both deductions from these figures and additions to them to provide a fair estimate of "labor's" income, we can assume on this basis that labor costs cannot be less than about two-thirds of total production costs and may run above three-quarters (depending upon our definition of labor). If we take the lower of these two estimates, and assume also that dollar profit margins would be unchanged, it is clear that an increase of 30 percent in wage costs all around the circle would mean an increase of nearly 20 percent in prices.

But such a change would mean that the dollar profit margin representing the income of investors, managers and the self-employed, would then have, say, only 84 percent as much purchasing power as it had before. The long-run effect of this would be to cause a diminution of investment and new enterprise compared with what it would otherwise have been, and consequent transfers of men from the lower ranks of the self-employed to the higher ranks of wage-earners, until the previous relationships had been approximately restored. But this is only another way of saying that a 30 percent increase in wages under the conditions assumed would eventually mean also a 30 percent increase in prices.

It does not necessarily follow that wage-earners would make no relative gains. They would make a relative gain, and other elements in the population would suffer a relative loss, *during the period of transition*. But it is improbable that this relative gain would mean an absolute gain. For the kind of change in the relationship of costs to prices contemplated here could hardly take place without bringing about unemployment and unbalanced, interrupted or reduced production. So that while labor might get a wider slice of a smaller pie, during this period of transition and adjustment to a new equilibrium, it may be doubted whether this would be greater in absolute size (and it might easily be less) than the previous narrower slice of a larger pie.

4

This brings us to the general meaning and effect of economic *equilibrium*. Equilibrium wages and prices are the wages and prices that equalize supply and demand. If, either through government or private coercion, an attempt is made to lift prices above their equilibrium level, demand is reduced and therefore production is reduced. If an attempt is made to push prices below their equilibrium level, the consequent reduction or wiping out of profits will mean a falling off of supply or less production. Therefore any attempt to force prices either above or below their equilibrium levels (which are the levels toward which a free market constantly tends to bring them) will act to reduce the volume of employment and production below what it would otherwise have been.

To return, then, to the doctrine that labor must get "enough to buy back the product." The national product, it should be obvious, is neither created nor bought by manufacturing labor alone. It is bought by everyone—by white collar workers, professional men, farmers, employers, big and little, by investors, grocers, butchers, owners of small drugstores and gasoline stations—by everybody, in short, who contributes toward making the product.

As to the prices, wages and profits that should determine the distribution of that product, the best prices are not the highest prices, but the prices that encourage the largest volume of production and the largest volume of sales. The best wage rates for labor are not the highest wage rates, but the wage rates that permit full production, full employment and the largest sustained payrolls. The best profits, from the standpoint not only of industry but of labor, are not the lowest profits, but the profits that encourage most people to become employers or to provide more employment than before.

If we try to run the economy for the benefit of a single group or class, we shall injure or destroy all groups, including the members of the very class for whose benefit we have been trying to run it. We must run the economy for everybody.

CHAPTER XXII

THE FUNCTION OF PROFITS

THE INDIGNATION SHOWN by many people today at the mention of the very word *profits* indicates how little understanding there is of the vital function that profits play in our economy. To increase our understanding, we shall go over again some of the ground already covered in chapter fifteen on the price system, but we shall view the subject from a different angle.

Profits actually do not bulk large in our total economy. The net income of incorporated business in the fifteen years from 1929 to 1943, to take some illustrative figures, averaged less than 5 percent of the total national income. Corporate profits after taxes in the five years from 1956 to 1960 averaged less than 6 percent of the national income. Corporate profits after taxes in the five years 1971 through 1975 also averaged less than 6 percent of the national income (in spite of the fact that, as a result of insufficient accounting adjustment for inflation, they were probably overstated).[10] Yet profits are the form of income toward which there is most hostility. It is significant that while there is a word *profiteer* to stigmatize those who make allegedly excessive profits, there is no such word as "wageer"—or "losseer." Yet the profits of the owner of a barbershop may average much less not merely than the salary of a motion picture star or the hired head of a steel corporation, but less even than the average wage for skilled labor.

The subject is clouded by all sorts of factual misconceptions. The total profits of General Motors, the greatest industrial corporation in the world, are taken as if they were typical rather than exceptional. Few people are acquainted with the mortality rates for business concerns. They do not know (to quote from the TNEC studies) that "should conditions of business averaging the experience of the last fifty years prevail, about seven of each ten grocery stores opening today will survive into their second year; only four of the ten may expect to celebrate their fourth birthday." They do not know that in every year from 1930 to 1938, in the income tax statistics, the number of corporations that showed a loss exceeded the number that showed a profit.

How much do profits, on the average, amount to?

This question is commonly answered by citing the kind of figures I presented at the beginning of this chapter — that corporate profits average less than 6 percent of the national income — or by pointing out that the average profits after income taxes of all manufacturing corporations are less than five cents per dollar of sales. (For the five years 1971 through 1975, for example, the figure was only 4.6 cents.)[11] But these official figures, though they fall far below popular notions of the size of profits, apply only to corporation results, calculated by conventional methods of accounting. No trustworthy estimate has been made that takes into account all kinds of activity, unincorporated as well as incorporated business, and a sufficient number of good and bad years. But some eminent economists believe that over a long period of years, after allowance is made for all losses, for a minimum "riskless" interest on invested capital, and for an imputed "reasonable" wage value of the services of people who run their own business, no net profit at all may be left over, and that there may even be a net loss. This is not at all because entrepreneurs (people who go into business for themselves) are intentional philanthropists, but because their optimism and self-confidence too often lead them into ventures that do not or cannot succeed.*

---

* Cf. Frank H. Knight, *Risk, Uncertainty and Profit* (1921). In any period in which there has been net capital accumulation, however, the presumption is strong that there must also have been overall net profits from previous investment.

It is clear, in any case, that any individual placing venture capital runs a risk not only of earning no return but of losing his whole principal. In the past it has been the lure of high profits in special firms or industries that has led him to take that great risk. But if profits are limited to a maximum of, say, 10 percent or some similar figure, while the risk of losing one's entire capital still exists, what is likely to be the effect on the profit incentive, and hence on employment and production? The World War II excess-profits tax showed what such a limit can do, even for a short period, in undermining efficiency.

Yet governmental policy almost everywhere today tends to assume that production will go on automatically, no matter what is done to discourage it. One of the greatest dangers to world production today still comes from government price-fixing policies. Not only do these policies put one item after another out of production by leaving no incentive to make it, but their long-run effect is to prevent a balance of production in accordance with the actual demands of consumers. When the economy is free, demand so acts that some branches of production make what some government officials regard as "excessive," "unreasonable," or even "obscene" profits. But that very fact not only causes every firm in that line to expand its production to the utmost, and to reinvest its profits in more machinery and more employment; it also attracts new investors and producers from everywhere, until production in that line is great enough to meet demand, and the profits in it again fall to (or below) the general average level.

In a free economy, in which wages, costs and prices are left to the free play of the competitive market, the prospect of profits decides what articles will be made, and in what quantities — and what articles will not be made at all. If there is no profit in making an article, it is a sign that the labor and capital devoted to its production are misdirected: the value of the resources that must be used up in making the article is greater than the value of the article itself.

One function of profits, in brief, is to guide and channel the factors of production so as to apportion the relative output of thousands of different commodities in accordance with demand. No bureaucrat, no matter how brilliant, can solve this problem arbitrarily. Free prices and free profits will maximize production and relieve shortages quicker than any other system. Arbitrarily fixed prices and arbitrarily limited profits can only prolong shortages and reduce production and employment.

The function of profits, finally, is to put constant and unremitting pressure on the head of every competitive business to introduce further economies and efficiencies, no matter to what stage these may already have been brought. In good times he does this to increase his profits further, in normal times he does it to keep ahead of his competitors, in bad times he may have to do it to survive at all. For profits may not only go to zero, they may quickly turn into losses; and a man will put forth greater efforts to save himself from ruin than he will merely to improve his position.

Contrary to a popular impression, profits are achieved not by raising prices, but by introducing economies and efficiencies that cut costs of production. It seldom happens (and unless there is a monopoly it never happens over a long period) that every firm in an industry makes a profit. The price charged by all firms for the same commodity or service must be the same; those who try to charge a higher price do not find buyers. Therefore the largest profits go to the firms that have achieved the lowest costs of production. These expand at the expense of the inefficient firms with higher costs. It is thus that the consumer and the public are served.

Profits, in short, resulting from the relationships of costs to prices, not only tell us which goods it is most economical to make, but which are the most economical ways to make them. These questions must be answered by a socialist system no less than by a capitalist one; they must be answered by any conceivable economic system; and for the overwhelming bulk of the commodities and services that are produced, the answers supplied by profit and loss under competitive free enterprise are incomparably superior to those that could be obtained by any other method.

I have been putting my emphasis on the tendency to reduce costs of production because this is the function of profit-and-loss that seems to be least appreciated. Greater profit goes, of course, to the man who makes a *better* mousetrap than his neighbor as well as to the man who makes one more efficiently. But the function of profit in rewarding and stimulating superior quality and innovation has always been recognized.

CHAPTER XXIII

THE MIRAGE OF INFLATION

I HAVE found it necessary to warn the reader from time to time that a certain result would necessarily follow from a certain policy "provided there is no inflation." In the chapters on public works and on credit I said that a study of the complications introduced by inflation would have to be deferred. But money and monetary policy form so intimate and sometimes so inextricable a part of every economic process that this separation, even for expository purposes, was very difficult and in the chapters on the effect of various government or union wage policies on employment, profits and production, some of the effects of differing monetary policies had to be considered immediately.

Before we consider what the consequences of inflation are in specific cases, we should consider what its consequences are in general. Even prior to that, it seems desirable to ask why inflation has been constantly resorted to, why it has had an immemorial popular appeal, and why its siren music has tempted one nation after another down the path to economic disaster.

The most obvious and yet the oldest and most stubborn error on which the appeal of inflation rests is that of confusing "money" with wealth. "That wealth consists in money, or in gold and silver," wrote Adam Smith more than two centuries ago "is a popular notion which naturally arises from the double function of money, as the instrument of commerce, and as the measure of value. . . . To grow rich is to get money, and wealth and money, in short, are, in common language, considered as in every respect synonymous."

Real wealth, of course, consists in what is produced and consumed: the food we eat, the clothes we wear, the houses we live in. It is railways and roads and motor cars; ships and planes and factories; schools and churches and theaters; pianos, paintings and books. Yet so powerful is the verbal ambiguity that confuses money with wealth, that even those who at times recognize the confusion will slide back into it in the course of their reasoning. Each man sees that if he personally had more money he could buy more things from others. If he had twice as much money he could buy twice as many things; if he had three times as much money he would be "worth" three times as much. And to many the conclusion seems obvious that if the government merely issued more money and distributed it to everybody, we should all be that much richer.

These are the most naive inflationists. There is a second group, less naive, who see that if the whole thing were as easy as that the government could solve all our problems merely by printing money. They sense that there must be a catch somewhere; so they would limit in some way the amount of additional money they would have the government issue. They would have it print just enough to make up some alleged "deficiency," or "gap."

Purchasing power is chronically deficient, they think, because industry somehow does not distribute enough money to producers to enable them to buy back, as consumers, the product that is made. There is a mysterious "leak" somewhere. One group "proves" it by equations. On one side of their equations they count an item only once; on the other side they unknowingly count the same item several times over. This produces an alarming gap between what they call "A payments" and what they call "A+B payments." So they found a movement, put on green uniforms, and insist that the government issue money or "credits" to make good the missing B payments.

The cruder apostles of "social credit" may seem ridiculous; but there are an indefinite number of schools of only slightly more sophisticated inflationists who have "scientific" plans to issue just enough additional money or credit to fill some alleged chronic or periodic deficiency, or gap, which they calculate in some other way.

2

The more knowing inflationists recognize that any substantial increase in the quantity of money will reduce the purchasing power of each individual monetary unit—in other words, that it will lead to an increase in commodity prices. But this does not disturb them. On the contrary, it is precisely why they want the inflation. Some of them argue that this result will improve the position of poor debtors as compared with rich creditors. Others think it will stimulate exports and discourage imports. Still others think it is an essential measure to cure a depression, to "start industry going again," and to achieve "full employment."[*]

There are innumerable theories concerning the way in which increased quantities of money (including bank credit) affect prices. On the one hand, as we have just seen, are those who imagine that the quantity of money could be increased by almost any amount without affecting prices. They merely see this increased money as a means of increasing everyone's "purchasing power," in the sense of enabling everybody to buy more goods than before. Either they never stop to remind themselves that people collectively cannot buy twice as much goods as before unless twice as much goods are produced, or they imagine that the only thing that holds down an indefinite increase in production is not a shortage of manpower, working hours or productive capacity, but merely a shortage of monetary demand: if people want the goods, they assume, and have the money to pay for them, the goods will almost automatically be produced.

----

[*] Stripped down to its essentials, this is the theory of the Keynesians. In *The Failure of the "New Economics"* (New Rochelle, N.Y.: Arlington House, 1959) I analyze this theory in detail.

On the other hand is the group—and it has included some eminent economists—that holds a rigid mechanical theory of the effect of the supply of money on commodity prices. All the money in a nation, as these theorists picture the matter, will be offered against all the goods. Therefore the value of the total quantity of money multiplied by its "velocity of circulation" must always be equal to the value of the total quantity of goods bought. Therefore, further (assuming no change in velocity of circulation), the value of the monetary unit must vary exactly and inversely with the amount put into circulation. Double the quantity of money and bank credit and you exactly double the "price level"; triple it, and you exactly triple the price level. Multiply the quantity of money n times, in short, and you must multiply the prices of goods n times.

There is not space here to explain all the fallacies in this plausible picture.[*] Instead we shall try to see just why and how an increase in the quantity of money raises prices.

An increased quantity of money comes into existence in a specific way. Let us say that it comes into existence because the government makes larger expenditures than it can or wishes to meet out of the proceeds of taxes (or from the sale of bonds paid for by the people out of real savings). Suppose, for example, that the government prints money to pay war contractors. Then the first effect of these expenditures will be to raise the prices of supplies used in war and to put additional money into the hands of the war contractors and their employees. (As, in our chapter on price-fixing, we deferred for the sake of simplicity some complications introduced by an inflation, so, in now considering inflation, we may pass over the complications introduced by an attempt at government price-fixing. When these are considered it will be

---

[*] The reader interested in an analysis of them should consult B. M. Anderson, *The Value of Money* (1917; new edition, 1936); Ludwig von Mises, *The Theory of Money and Credit* (American editions, 1935, 1953), or the present writer's *The Inflation Crisis, and How to Resolve It* (New Rochelle, NY,: Arlington House, 1978).

found that they do not change the essential analysis. They lead merely to a sort of backed-up or "repressed" inflation that reduces or conceals some of the earlier consequences at the expense of aggravating the later ones.)

The war contractors and their employees, then, will have higher money incomes. They will spend them for the particular goods and services they want. The sellers of these goods and services will be able to raise their prices because of this increased demand. Those who have the increased money income will be willing to pay these higher prices rather than do without the goods; for they will have more money, and a dollar will have a smaller subjective value in the eyes of each of them.

Let us call the war contractors and their employees group A, and those from whom they directly buy their added goods and services group B. Group B, as a result of higher sales and prices, will now in turn buy more goods and services from a still further group, C. Group C in turn will be able to raise its prices and will have more income to spend on group D, and so on, until the rise in prices and money incomes has covered virtually the whole nation. When the process has been completed, nearly everybody will have a higher income measured in terms of money. But (assuming that production of goods and services has not increased) prices of goods and services will have increased correspondingly. The nation will be no richer than before.

This does not mean, however, that everyone's relative or absolute wealth and income will remain the same as before. On the contrary, the process of inflation is certain to affect the fortunes of one group differently from those of another. The first groups to receive the additional money will benefit the most. The money incomes of group A, for example, will have increased before prices have increased, so that they will be able to buy almost a proportionate increase in goods. The money incomes of group B will advance later, when prices have already increased somewhat; but group B will be better off in terms of goods. Meanwhile, however, the groups that have still had no advance whatever in their money incomes will find themselves compelled to pay higher prices for the things they buy, which means that they will be obliged to get along on a lower standard of living than before.

We may clarify the process further by a hypothetical set of figures. Suppose we divide the community arbitrarily into four main groups of producers, A, B, C and D, who get the money income benefit of the inflation in that order. Then when money incomes of group A have already increased 30 percent, the prices of the things they purchase have not yet increased at all. By the time money incomes of group B have increased 20 percent, prices have still increased an average of only 10 percent. When money incomes of group C have increased only 10 percent, however, prices have already gone up 15 percent. And when money incomes of group D have not yet increased at all, the average prices they have to pay for the things they buy have gone up 20 percent. In other words, the gains of the first groups of producers to benefit by higher prices or wages from the inflation are necessarily at the expense of the losses suffered (as consumers) by the last groups of producers that are able to raise their prices or wages.

It may be that, if the inflation is brought to a halt after a few years, the final result will be, say, an average increase of 25 percent in money incomes, and an average increase in prices of an equal amount, both of which are fairly distributed among all groups. But this will not cancel out the gains and losses of the transition period. Group D, for example, even though its own incomes and prices have at last advanced 25 percent, will be able to buy only as much goods and services as before the inflation started. It will never compensate for its losses during that period when its income and prices had not risen at all, though it had to pay up to 30 percent more for the goods and services it bought from the other producing groups in the community, A, B and C.

3

So inflation turns out to be merely one more example of our central lesson. It may indeed bring benefits for a short time to favored groups, but only at the expense of others. And in the long run it brings ruinous consequences to the whole community. Even a relatively mild inflation distorts the structure of production. It leads to the overexpansion of some industries at the expense of others. This involves a misapplication and waste of capital. When the inflation collapses, or is brought to a halt, the misdirected capital investment—whether in the form of machines, factories or office buildings—cannot yield an adequate return and loses the greater part of its value.

Nor is it possible to bring inflation to a smooth and gentle stop, and so avert a subsequent depression. It is not even possible to halt an inflation, once embarked upon, at some preconceived point, or when prices have achieved a previously agreed upon level; for both political and economic forces will have got out of hand. You cannot make an argument for a 25 percent advance in prices by inflation without someone's contending that the argument is twice as good for an advance of 50 percent, and someone else's adding that it is four times as good for an advance of 100 percent. The political pressure groups that have benefited from the inflation will insist upon its continuance.

It is impossible, moreover, to control the value of money under inflation. For, as we have seen, the causation is never a merely mechanical one. You cannot, for example, say in advance that a 100 percent increase in the quantity of money will mean a 50 percent fall in the value of the monetary unit. The value of money, as we have seen, depends upon the subjective valuations of the people who hold it. And those valuations do not depend solely on the quantity of it that each person holds. They depend also on the *quality* of the money. In wartime the value of a nation's monetary unit, not on the gold standard, will rise on the foreign exchanges with victory and fall with defeat, regardless of changes in its quantity. The present valuation will often depend upon what people expect the *future* quantity of money to be. And, as with commodities on the speculative exchanges, each person's valuation of money is affected not only by what he thinks its value is but by what he thinks is going to be *everybody else's* valuation of money.

All this explains why, when hyperinflation has once set in, the value of the monetary unit drops at a far faster rate than the quantity of money either is or can be increased. When this stage is reached, the disaster is nearly complete; and the scheme is bankrupt.

4

Yet the ardor for inflation never dies. It would almost seem as if no country is capable of profiting from the experience of another and no generation of learning from the sufferings of its forebears. Each generation and country follows the same mirage. Each grasps for the same Dead Sea fruit that turns to dust and ashes in its mouth. For it is the nature of inflation to give birth to a thousand illusions.

In our own day the most persistent argument put forward for inflation is that it will "get the wheels of industry turning," that it will save us from the irretrievable losses of stagnation and idleness and bring "full employment." This argument in its cruder form rests on the immemorial confusion between money and real wealth. It assumes that new "purchasing power" is being brought into existence, and that the effects of this new purchasing power multiply themselves in ever-widening circles, like the ripples caused by a stone thrown into a pond. The real purchasing power for goods, however, as we have seen, consists of other goods. It cannot be wondrously increased merely by printing more pieces of paper called dollars. Fundamentally what happens in an exchange economy is that the things that A produces are exchanged for the things that B produces.[*]

---

[*] Cf. John Stuart Mill, *Principles of Political Economy* (Book 3, Chap. 14, par. 2); Alfred Marshall, *Principles of Economics* (Book VI, Chap. XIII, sec. 10); Benjamin M. Anderson, "A Refutation of Keynes' Attack on the Doctrine that

What inflation really does is to change the relationships of prices and costs. The most important change it is designed to bring about is to raise commodity prices in relation to wage rates, and so to restore business profits, and encourage a resumption of output at the points where idle resources exist, by restoring a workable relationship between prices and costs of production.

It should be immediately clear that this could be brought about more directly and honestly by a reduction in unworkable wage rates. But the more sophisticated proponents of inflation believe that this is now politically impossible. Sometimes they go further, and charge that all proposals under any circumstances to reduce particular wage rates directly in order to reduce unemployment are "antilabor." But what they are themselves proposing, stated in bald terms, is to *deceive* labor by reducing *real* wage rates (that is, wage rates in terms of purchasing power) through an increase in prices.

What they forget is that labor has itself become sophisticated; that the big unions employ labor economists who know about index numbers, and that labor is not deceived. The policy, therefore, under present conditions, seems unlikely to accomplish either its economic or its political aims. For it is precisely the most powerful unions, whose wage rates are most likely to be in need of correction, that will insist that their wage rates be raised at least in proportion to any increase in the cost-of-living index. The unworkable relationships between prices and key wage rates, if the insistence of the powerful unions prevails, will remain. The wage rate structure, in fact, may become even more distorted; for the great mass of unorganized workers, whose wage rates even before the inflation were not out of line (and may even have been unduly

---

Aggregate Supply Creates Aggregate Demand," in *Financing American Prosperity* by a symposium of economists. Cf. also the symposium edited by the present author: *The Critics of Keynesian Economics* (New Rochelle, N.Y.: Arlington House, 1960).

depressed through union exclusionism), will be penalized further during the transition by the rise in prices.

5

The more sophisticated advocates of inflation, in brief, are disingenuous. They do not state their case with complete candor; and they end by deceiving even themselves. They begin to talk of paper money, like the more naive inflationists, as if it were itself a form of wealth that could be created at will on the printing press. They even solemnly discuss a "multiplier," by which every dollar printed and spent by the government becomes magically the equivalent of several dollars added to the wealth of the country.

In brief, they divert both the public attention and their own from the real causes of any existing depression. For the real causes, most of the time, are maladjustments within the wage-cost-price structure: maladjustments between wages and prices, between prices of raw materials and prices of finished goods, or between one price and another or one wage and another. At some point these maladjustments have removed the incentive to produce, or have made it actually impossible for production to continue; and through the organic interdependence of our exchange economy, depression spreads. Not until these maladjustments are corrected can full production and employment be resumed.

True, inflation may sometimes correct them; but it is a heady and dangerous method. It makes its corrections not openly and honestly, but by the use of illusion. Inflation, indeed, throws a veil of illusion over every economic process. It confuses and deceives almost everyone, including even those who suffer by it. We are all accustomed to measuring our income and wealth in terms of money. The mental habit is so strong that even professional economists and statisticians cannot consistently break it. It is not easy to see relationships always in terms of real goods and real welfare. Who among us does not feel richer and prouder when he is told that our national income has doubled (in terms of dollars, of course) compared with some preinflationary period? Even the clerk who used to get $75 a week and now gets $120 thinks that he must be in some way better off, though it costs him twice as much to live as it did when he was getting $75. He is of course not blind to the rise in the cost of living. But neither is he as fully aware of his real position as he would have been if his cost of living had not changed and if his money salary had been reduced to give him the same reduced purchasing power that he now has, in spite of his salary increase, because of higher prices. Inflation is the autosuggestion, the hypnotism, the anesthetic, that has dulled the pain of the operation for him. Inflation is the opium of the people.

6

And this is precisely its political function. It is because inflation confuses everything that it is so consistently resorted to by our modern "planned economy" governments. We saw in chapter four, to take but one example, that the belief that public works necessarily create new jobs is false. If the money was raised by taxation, we saw, then for every dollar that the government spent on public works one less dollar was spent by the taxpayers to meet their own wants, and for every public job created one private job was destroyed.

But suppose the public works are not paid for from the proceeds of taxation? Suppose they are paid for by deficit financing—that is, from the proceeds of government borrowing or from resort to the printing press? Then the result just described does not seem to take place. The public works seem to be created out of "new" purchasing power. You cannot say that the purchasing power has been taken away from the taxpayers. For the moment the nation seems to have got something for nothing.

But now, in accordance with our lesson, let us look at the longer consequences. The borrowing must some day be repaid. The government cannot keep piling up debt indefinitely; for if it tries, it will some day become bankrupt. As Adam Smith observed in 1776:

> When national debts have once been accumulated to a certain degree, there is scarce, I believe, a single instance of their having been fairly and completely paid. The liberation of the public revenue, if it has even been brought about at all, has always been brought about by a bankruptcy; sometimes by an avowed one, but always by a real one, though frequently by a pretended payment.

Yet when the government comes to repay the debt it has accumulated for public works, it must necessarily tax more heavily than it spends. In this later period, therefore, it must necessarily destroy more jobs than it creates. The extra-heavy taxation then required does not merely take away purchasing power; it also lowers or destroys incentives to production, and so reduces the total wealth and income of the country.

The only escape from this conclusion is to assume (as of course the apostles of spending always do) that the politicians in power will spend money only in what would otherwise have been depressed or "deflationary" periods, and will promptly pay the debt off in what would otherwise have been boom or "inflationary" periods. This is a beguiling fiction, but unfortunately the politicians in power have never acted that way. Economic forecasting, moreover, is so precarious, and the political pressures at work are of such a nature, that governments are unlikely ever to act that way. Deficit spending, once embarked upon, creates powerful vested interests which demand its continuance under all conditions.

If no honest attempt is made to pay off the accumulated debt, and resort is had to outright inflation instead, then the results follow that we have already described. For the country as a whole cannot get anything without paying for it. Inflation itself is a form of taxation. It is perhaps the worst possible form, which usually bears hardest on those least able to pay. On the assumption that inflation affected everyone and everything evenly (which, we have seen, is never true), it would be tantamount to a flat sales tax of the same percentage on all commodities, with the rate as high on bread and milk as on diamonds and furs. Or it might be thought of as equivalent to a flat tax of the same percentage, without exemptions, on everyone's income. It is a tax not only on every individual's expenditures, but on his savings account and life insurance. It is, in fact, a flat capital levy, without exemptions, in which the poor man pays as high a percentage as the rich man.

But the situation is even worse than this, because, as we have seen, inflation does not and cannot affect everyone evenly. Some suffer more than others. The poor are usually more heavily taxed by inflation, in percentage terms, than the rich, for they do not have the same means of protecting themselves by speculative purchases of real equities. Inflation is a kind of tax that is out of control of the tax authorities. It strikes wantonly in all directions. The rate of tax imposed by inflation is not a fixed one: it cannot be determined in advance. We know what it is today; we do not know what it will be tomorrow; and tomorrow we shall not know what it will be on the day after.

Like every other tax, inflation acts to determine the individual and business policies we are all forced to follow. It discourages all prudence and thrift. It encourages squandering, gambling, reckless waste of all kinds. It often makes it more profitable to speculate than to produce. It tears apart the whole fabric of stable economic relationships. Its inexcusable injustices drive men toward desperate remedies. It plants the seeds of fascism and communism. It leads men to demand totalitarian controls. It ends invariably in bitter disillusion and collapse.

CHAPTER XXIV

THE ASSAULT ON SAVING

FROM TIME IMMEMORIAL proverbial wisdom has taught the vir-
tues of saving, and warned against the consequences of prodigality
and waste. This proverbial wisdom has reflected the common
ethical as well as the merely prudential judgments of mankind.
But there have always been squanderers, and there have apparently
always been theorists to rationalize their squandering.

The classical economists, refuting the fallacies of their own day,
showed that the saving policy that was in the best interests of the
individual was also in the best interests of the nation. They showed
that the rational saver, in making provision for his future, was not
hurting, but helping, the whole community. But today the ancient
virtue of thrift, as well as its defense by the classical economists, is
once more under attack, for allegedly new reasons, while the
opposite doctrine of spending is in fashion.

In order to make the fundamental issue as clear as possible, we
cannot do better, I think, than to start with the classic example used
by Bastiat. Let us imagine two brothers, then, one a spendthrift and
the other a prudent man, each of whom has inherited a sum to
yield him an income of $50,000 a year. We shall disregard the
income tax, and the question whether both brothers really ought
to work for a living or give most of their income to charity, because
such questions are irrelevant to our present purpose.

Alvin, then, the first brother, is a lavish spender. He spends not
only by temperament, but on principle. He is a disciple (to go no
further back) of Rodbertus, who declared in the middle of the
nineteenth century that capitalists "must expend their income to

the last penny in comforts and luxuries," for if they "determine to save . . . goods accumulate, and part of the workmen will have no work."[*] Alvin is always seen at the night clubs; he tips handsomely; he maintains a pretentious establishment, with plenty of servants; he has a couple of chauffeurs, and doesn't stint himself in the number of cars he owns; he keeps a racing stable; he runs a yacht; he travels; he loads his wife down with diamond bracelets and fur coats; he gives expensive and useless presents to his friends.

To do all this he has to dig into his capital. But what of it? If saving is a sin, dissaving must be a virtue; and in any case he is simply making up for the harm being done by the saving of his pinchpenny brother Benjamin.

It need hardly be said that Alvin is a great favorite with the hat check girls, the waiters, the restaurateurs, the furriers, the jewelers, the luxury establishments of all kinds. They regard him as a public benefactor. Certainly it is obvious to everyone that he is giving employment and spreading his money around.

Compared with him brother Benjamin is much less popular. He is seldom seen at the jewelers, the furriers or the night clubs, and he does not call the head waiters by their first names. Whereas Alvin spends not only the full $50,000 income each year but is digging into capital besides, Benjamin lives much more modestly and spends only about $25,000. Obviously, think the people who see only what hits them in the eye, he is providing less than half as much employment as Alvin, and the other $25,000 is as useless as if it did not exist.

But let us see what Benjamin actually does with this other $25,000. He does not let it pile up in his pocketbook, his bureau drawers, or in his safe. He either deposits it in a bank or he invests it. If he puts it either into a commercial or a savings bank, the bank either lends it to going businesses on short term for working capital, or uses it to buy securities. In other words, Benjamin invests his

---

[*] Karl Rodbertus, *Overproduction and Crises* (1850), p. 51.

money either directly or indirectly. But when money is invested it is used to buy or build capital goods—houses or office buildings or factories or ships or trucks or machines. Any one of these projects puts as much money into circulation and gives as much employment as the same amount of money spent directly on consumption.

"Saving," in short, in the modern world, is only another form of spending. The usual difference is that the money is turned over to someone else to spend on means to increase production. So far as giving employment is concerned, Benjamin's "saving" and spending combined give as much as Alvin's spending alone, and put as much money in circulation. The chief difference is that the employment provided by Alvin's spending can be seen by anyone with one eye; but it is necessary to look a little more carefully, and to think a moment, to recognize that every dollar of Benjamin's saving gives as much employment as every dollar that Alvin throws around.

A dozen years roll by. Alvin is broke. He is no longer seen in the night clubs and at the fashionable shops; and those whom he formerly patronized, when they speak of him, refer to him as something of a fool. He writes begging letters to Benjamin. And Benjamin, who continues about the same ratio of spending to saving, not only provides more jobs than ever, because his income, through investment, has grown, but through his investment he has helped to provide better-paying and more productive jobs. His capital wealth and income are greater. He has, in brief, added to the nation's productive capacity; Alvin has not.

2

So many fallacies have grown up about saving in recent years that they cannot all be answered by our example of the two brothers. It is necessary to devote some further space to them. Many stem from confusions so elementary as to seem incredible, particularly when found in the works of economic writers of wide repute. The word *saving*, for example, is used sometimes to mean mere *hoarding* of money, and sometimes to mean *investment*, with no clear distinction, consistently maintained, between the two uses.

Mere hoarding of hand-to-hand money, if it takes place irrationally, causelessly, and on a large scale, is in most economic situations harmful. But this sort of hoarding is extremely rare. Something that looks like this, but should be carefully distinguished from it, often occurs *after* a downturn in business has got under way. Consumptive spending and investment are then *both* contracted. Consumers reduce their buying. They do this partly, indeed, because they fear they may lose their jobs, and they wish to conserve their resources: they have contracted their buying not because they wish to consume less but because they wish to make sure that their power to consume will be extended over a longer period if they do lose their jobs.

But consumers reduce their buying for another reason. Prices of goods have probably fallen, and they fear a further fall. If they defer spending, they believe they will get more for their money. They do not wish to have their resources in goods that are falling in value, but in money which they expect (relatively) to rise in value.

The same expectation prevents them from investing. They have lost their confidence in the profitability of business; or at least they believe that if they wait a few months they can buy stocks or bonds cheaper. We may think of them either as refusing to hold goods that may fall in value on their hands, or as holding money itself for a rise.

It is a misnomer to call this temporary refusal to buy "saving." It does not spring from the same motives as normal saving. And it is a still more serious error to say that this sort of "saving" is the *cause* of depressions. It is, on the contrary, the *consequence* of depressions.

It is true that this refusal to buy may intensify and prolong a depression. At times when there is capricious government intervention in business, and when business does not know what the government is going to do next, uncertainty is created. Profits are not reinvested. Firms and individuals allow cash balances to accumulate in their banks. They keep larger reserves against contingencies. This hoarding of cash may seem like a cause of a subsequent slowdown in business activity. The real cause, how-ever, is the uncertainty brought about by the government policies. The larger cash balances of firms and individuals are merely one link in the chain of consequences from that uncertainty. To blame "excessive saving" for the business decline would be like blaming a fall in the price of apples not on a bumper crop but on the people who refuse to pay more for apples.

But when once people have decided to deride a practice or an institution, any argument against it, no matter how illogical, is considered good enough. It is said that the various consumers' goods industries are built on the expectation of a certain demand, and that if people take to saving they will disappoint this expecta-tion and start a depression. This assertion rests primarily on the error we have already examined—that of forgetting that what is saved on consumers' goods is spent on capital goods, and that "saving" does not necessarily mean even a dollar's contraction in *total* spending. The only element of truth in the contention is that *any* change that is *sudden* may be unsettling. It would be just as unsettling if consumers suddenly switched their demand from one consumers' good to another. It would be even more unsettling if former savers suddenly switched their demand from capital goods to consumers' goods

Still another objection is made against saving. It is said to be just downright silly. The nineteenth century is derided for its supposed inculcation of the doctrine that mankind through saving should go on baking itself a larger and larger cake without ever eating the cake. This picture of the process is itself naive and childish. It can best be disposed of, perhaps, by putting before ourselves a some-what more realistic picture of what actually takes place.

Let us picture to ourselves, then, a nation that collectively saves every year about 20 percent of all it produces in that year. This figure greatly overstates the amount of net saving that has occurred historically in the United States,[*] but it is a round figure that is easily handled, and it gives the benefit of every doubt to those who believe that we have been "oversaving."

Now as a result of this annual saving and investment, the total annual production of the country will increase each year. (To isolate the problem we are ignoring for the moment booms, slumps, or other fluctuations.) Let us say that this annual increase in production is 2.5 percentage points. (Percentage points are taken instead of a compounded percentage merely to simplify the arithmetic.) The picture that we get for an eleven-year period, say, would then run something like this in terms of index numbers:

Year	Total Production	Consumers' Goods Production	Capital Goods Production
First	100	80	20[†]
Second	102.5	82	20.5
Third	105	84	21
Fourth	107.5	86	21.5
Fifth	110	88	22
Sixth	112.5	90	22.5
Seventh	115	92	23
Eighth	117.5	94	23.5
Ninth	120	96	24
Tenth	122.5	98	24.5
Eleventh	125	100	25

---

[*] Historically 20 percent would represent approximately the *gross* amount of the gross national product devoted each year to capital formation (excluding consumers' equipment). When allowance is made for capital consumption. however, *net* annual savings have been closer to 12 percent. Cf. George Terborgh, *The Bogey of Economic Maturity* (1945). For 1977 domestic investment was officially estimated at 16 percent of th/ product.

[†] This of course assumes the process of saving and investn/ already under way at the same rate.

The first thing to be noticed about this table is that total production increases each year *because of the saving*, and would not have increased without it. (It is possible no doubt to imagine that improvements and new inventions merely in *replaced* machinery and other capital goods of a value no greater than the old would increase the national productivity; but this increase would amount to very little and the argument in any case assumes enough prior investment to have made the existing machinery possible.) The saving has been used year after year to increase the quantity or improve the quality of existing machinery, and so to increase the nation's output of goods. There is, it is true (if that for some strange reason is considered an objection), a larger and larger "cake" each year. Each year, it is true, not *all* of the currently produced cake is consumed. But there is no irrational or cumulative restraint. For each year a larger and larger cake is in fact consumed; until, at the end of eleven years (in our illustration), the annual consumers' cake alone is equal to the combined consumers' and producers' cakes of the first year. Moreover, the capital equipment, the ability to produce goods, is itself 25 percent greater than in the first year.

Let us observe a few other points. The fact that 20 percent of the national income goes each year for saving does not upset the consumers' goods industries in the least. If they sold only the 80 units they produced in the first year (and there were no rise in prices caused by unsatisfied demand) they would certainly not be foolish enough to build their production plans on the assumption that they were going to sell 100 units in the second year. The consumers' goods industries, in other words, are *already geared* to the assumption that the past situation in regard to the rate of savings will continue. Only an unexpected *sudden and substantial increase* in savings would unsettle them and leave them with unsold goods.

But the same unsettlement, as we have already observed, would be caused in the *capital* goods industries by a sudden and substantial *decrease* in savings. If money that would previously have been used for savings were thrown into the purchase of consumers' goods, it would not increase employment but merely lead to an increase in the price of consumption goods and to a decrease in the price of capital goods. Its first effect on net balance would be to force shifts in employment and temporarily to *decrease* employment by its effect on the capital goods industries. And its long-run effect would be to reduce production below the level that would otherwise have been achieved.

3

The enemies of saving are not through. They begin by drawing a distinction, which is proper enough, between "savings" and "investment." But then they start to talk as if the two were independent variables and as if it were merely an accident that they should ever equal each other. These writers paint a portentous picture. On the one side are savers automatically, pointlessly, stupidly continuing to save; on the other side are limited "investment opportunities" that cannot absorb this saving. The result, alas, is stagnation. The only solution, they declare, is for the government to expropriate these stupid and harmful savings and to invent its own projects, even if these are only useless ditches or pyramids, to use up the money and provide employment.

There is so much that is false in this picture and "solution" that we can here point only to some of the main fallacies. Savings can exceed investment only by the amounts that are actually *hoarded in cash.*[*] Few people nowadays, in a modern industrial community, hoard coins and bills in stockings or under mattresses. To the small extent that this may occur, it has already been reflected in the production plans of business and in the price level. It is not

---

[*] Many of the differences between economists in the diverse views now expressed on this subject are merely the result of differences in definition. *Savings* and *investment* may be so defined as to be identical, and therefore necessarily equal. Here I am choosing to define *savings* in terms of money and investment in terms of goods. This corresponds roughly with the common use of the words, which is, however, not consistent.

ordinarily even cumulative: dishoarding, as eccentric recluses die and their hoards are discovered and dissipated, probably offsets new hoarding. In fact, the whole amount involved is probably insignificant in its effect on business activity.

If money is kept either in savings banks or commercial banks, as we have already seen, the banks are eager to lend and invest it. They cannot afford to have idle funds. The only thing that will cause people generally to try to increase their holdings of cash, or that will cause banks to hold funds idle and lose the interest on them, is, as we have seen, either fear that prices of goods are going to fall or the fear of banks that they will be taking too great a risk with their principal. But this means that signs of a depression have already appeared, and have caused the hoarding, rather than that the hoarding has started the depression.

Apart from this negligible hoarding of cash, then (and even this exception might be thought of as a direct "investment" in money itself) savings and investment are brought into equilibrium with each other in the same way that the supply of and demand for any commodity are brought into equilibrium. For we may define savings and investment as constituting respectively the supply of and demand for new capital. And just as the supply of and demand for any other commodity are equalized by price, so the supply of and demand for capital are equalized by interest rates. The interest rate is merely the special name for the price of loaned capital. It is a price like any other.

This whole subject has been so appallingly confused in recent years by complicated sophistries and disastrous governmental policies based upon them that one almost despairs of getting back to common sense and sanity about it. There is a psychopathic fear of "excessive" interest rates. It is argued that if interest rates are too high it will not be profitable for industry to borrow and invest in new plants and machines. This argument has been so effective that governments everywhere in recent decades have pursued artificial "cheap-money" policies. But the argument, in its concern with increasing the demand for capital, overlooks the effect of these policies on the supply of capital. It is one more example of the fallacy of looking at the effects of a policy only on one group and forgetting the effects on another.

If interest rates are artificially kept too low in relation to risks, there will be a reduction in both saving and lending. The cheap-money proponents believe that saving goes on automatically, regardless of the interest rate, because the sated rich have nothing else that they can do with their money. They do not stop to tell us at precisely what personal income level a man saves a fixed minimum amount regardless of the rate of interest or the risk at which he can lend it.

The fact is that, though the volume of saving of the very rich is doubtless affected much less proportionately than that of the moderately well-off by changes in the interest rate, practically everyone's saving is affected in some degree. To argue, on the basis of an extreme example, that the volume of real savings would not be reduced by a substantial reduction in the interest rate, is like arguing that the total production of sugar would not be reduced by a substantial fall of its price because the efficient, low-cost producers would still raise as much as before. The argument overlooks the marginal saver, and even, indeed, the great majority of savers.

The effect of keeping interest rates artificially low, in fact, is eventually the same as that of keeping any other price below the natural market. It increases demand and reduces supply. It increases the demand for capital and reduces the supply of real capital. It creates economic distortions. It is true, no doubt, that an artificial reduction in the interest rate encourages increased borrowing. It tends, in fact, to encourage highly speculative ventures that cannot continue except under the artificial conditions that gave them birth. On the supply side, the artificial reduction of interest rates discourages normal thrift, saving, and investment. It reduces the accumulation of capital. It slows down that increase in productivity, that "economic growth," that "progressives" profess to be so eager to promote.

The money rate can, indeed, be kept artificially low only by continuous new injections of currency or bank credit in place of real savings. This can create the illusion of more capital just as the addition of water can create the illusion of more milk. But it is a policy of continuous inflation. It is obviously a process involving cumulative danger. The money rate will rise and a crisis will develop if the inflation is reversed, or merely brought to a halt, or even continued at a diminished rate.

It remains to be pointed out that while new injections of currency or bank credit can at first, and temporarily, bring about lower interest rates, persistence in this device must eventually *raise* interest rates. It does so because new injections of money tend to lower the purchasing power of money. Lenders then come to realize that the money they lend today will buy less a year from now, say, when they get it back. Therefore to the normal interest rate they add a premium to compensate them for this expected loss in their money's purchasing power. This premium can be high, depending on the extent of the expected inflation. Thus the annual interest rate on British treasury bills rose to 14 percent in 1976; Italian government bonds yielded 16 percent in 1977; and the discount rate of the central bank of Chile soared to 75 percent in 1974. Cheap-money policies, in short, eventually bring about far more violent oscillations in business than those they are designed to remedy or prevent.

If no effort is made to tamper with money rates through inflationary governmental policies, increased savings create their own demand by lowering interest rates in a natural manner. The greater supply of savings seeking investment forces savers to accept lower rates. But lower rates also mean that more enterprises can afford to borrow because their prospective profit on the new machines or plants they buy with the proceeds seems likely to exceed what they have to pay for the borrowed funds.

4

We come now to the last fallacy about saving with which I intend to deal. This is the frequent assumption that there is a fixed limit to the amount of new capital that can be absorbed, or even that the limit of capital expansion has already been reached. It is incredible that such a view could prevail even among the ignorant, let alone that it could be held by any trained economist. Almost the whole wealth of the modern world, nearly everything that distinguishes it from the preindustrial world of the seventeenth century, consists of its accumulated capital.

This capital is made up in part of many things that might better be called consumers' durable goods—automobiles, refrigerators, furniture, schools, colleges, churches, libraries, hospitals and above all private homes. Never in the history of the world has there been enough of these. Even if there were enough homes from a purely numerical point of view, *qualitative* improvements are possible and desirable without definite limit in all but the very best houses.

The second part of capital is what we may call capital proper. It consists of the tools of production, including everything from the crudest axe, knife or plow to the finest machine tool, the greatest electric generator or cyclotron, or the most wonderfully equipped factory. Here, too, quantitatively and especially qualitatively, there is no limit to the expansion that is possible and desirable. There will not be a "surplus" of capital until the most backward country is as well equipped technologically as the most advanced, until the most inefficient factory in America is brought abreast of the factory with the latest and finest equipment, and until the most modern tools of production have reached a point where human ingenuity is at a dead end, and can improve them no further. As long as any of these conditions remains unfulfilled, there will be indefinite room for more capital.

But how can the additional capital be "absorbed"? How can it be "paid for"? If it is set aside and saved, it will absorb itself and pay for itself. For producers invest in new capital goods—that is, they buy new and better and more ingenious tools—because these tools *reduce costs of production.* They either bring into existence goods that completely unaided hand labor could not bring into existence at all (and this now includes most of the goods around us—books, typewriters, automobiles, locomotives, suspension bridges); or they increase enormously the quantities in which these can be produced; or (and this is merely saying these things in a different way) they reduce *unit* costs of production. And as there is no assignable limit to the extent to which unit costs of production can be reduced—until everything can be produced at no cost at all—there is no assignable limit to the amount of new capital that can be absorbed.

The steady reduction of unit costs of production by the addition of new capital does either one of two things, or both. It reduces the costs of goods to consumers, and it increases the wages of the labor that uses the new equipment because it increases the productive power of that labor. Thus a new machine benefits both the people who work on it directly and the great body of consumers. In the case of consumers we may say either that it supplies them with more and better goods for the same money, or, what is the same thing, that it increases their real incomes. In the case of the workers who use the new machines it increases their real wages in a double way by increasing their money wages as well. A typical illustration is the automobile business. The American automobile industry pays the highest wages in the world, and among the very highest even in America. Yet (until about 1960) American motorcar makers could undersell the rest of the world, because their unit cost was lower. And the secret was that the capital used in making American automobiles was greater per worker and per car than anywhere else in the world.

And yet there are people who think we have reached the end of this process,[*] and still others who think that even if we haven't, the world is foolish to go on saving and adding to its stock of capital.

It should not be difficult to decide, after our analysis, with whom the real folly lies.

---

[*] For a statistical refutation of this fallacy consult George Terborgh, *The Bogey of Economic Maturity* (1945). The "stagnationists" whom Dr. Terborgh was refuting have been succeeded by the Galbraithians with a similar doctrine.

(It is true that the U. S. has been losing its world economic leadership in recent years, but because of our own anticapitalist governmental policies, not because of "economic maturity.")

CHAPTER XXV

THE LESSON RESTATED

ECONOMICS, as we have now seen again and again, is a science of recognizing *secondary* consequences. It is also a science of seeing *general* consequences. It is the science of tracing the effects of some proposed or existing policy not only on some *special* interest *in the short run*, but on the *general* interest *in the long run*.

This is the lesson that has been the special concern of this book. We stated it first in skeleton form, and then put flesh and skin on it through more than a score of practical applications.

But in the course of specific illustration we have found hints of other general lessons; and we should do well to state these lessons to ourselves more clearly.

In seeing that economics is a science of tracing consequences, we must have become aware that, like logic and mathematics, it is a science of recognizing inevitable implications.

We may illustrate this by an elementary equation in algebra. Suppose we say that if $x = 5$ then $x + y = 12$. The "solution" to this equation is that y equals 7; but this is so precisely because the calculation *tells* us in effect that y equals 7. It does not make that assertion directly, but it inevitably implies it.

What is true of this elementary equation is true of the most complicated and abstruse equations encountered in mathematics. *The answer already lies in the statement of the problem*. It must, it is true, be "worked out." The result, it is true, may sometimes come to the man who works out the equation as a stunning surprise. He may even have a sense of discovering something entirely new—a thrill like that of "some watcher of the skies, when a new planet swims into his ken." His sense of discovery may be justified by the theoretical or practical consequences of his answer. Yet the answer was already contained in the formulation of the problem. It was merely not recognized at once. For mathematics reminds us that inevitable implications are not necessarily obvious implications.

All this is equally true of economics. In this respect economics might be compared also to engineering. When an engineer has a problem, he must first determine all the facts bearing on that problem. If he designs a bridge to span two points, he must first know the exact distance between these two points, their precise topographical nature, the maximum load his bridge will be designed to carry, the tensile and compressive strength of the steel or other material of which the bridge is to be built, and the stresses and strains to which it may be subjected. Much of this factual research has already been done for him by others. His predecessors, also, have already evolved elaborate mathematical equations by which, knowing the strength of his materials and the stresses to which they will be subjected, he can determine the necessary diameter, shape, number and structure of his towers, cables and girders.

In the same way the economist, assigned a practical problem, must know both the essential facts of that problem and the valid deductions to be drawn from those facts. The deductive side of economics is no less important than the factual. One can say of it what Santayana says of logic (and what could be equally well said of mathematics), that it "traces the radiation of truth," so that "when one term of a logical system is known to describe a fact, the whole system attaching to that term becomes, as it were, incandescent."[*]

Now few people recognize the necessary implications of the economic statements they are constantly making. When they say that the way to economic salvation is to increase credit, it is just as

---

[*] George Santayana, *The Realm of Truth* (1938), p. 16.

if they said that the way to economic salvation is to increase debt: these are different names for the same thing seen from opposite sides. When they say that the way to prosperity is to increase farm prices, it is like saying that the way to prosperity is to make food dearer for the city worker. When they say that the way to national wealth is to pay out governmental subsidies, they are in effect saying that the way to national wealth is to increase taxes. When they make it a main objective to increase exports, most of them do not realize that they necessarily make it a main objective ultimately to increase imports. When they say, under nearly all conditions, that the way to recovery is to increase wage rates, they have found only another way of saying that the way to recovery is to increase costs of production.

It does not necessarily follow, because each of these propositions, like a coin, has its reverse side, or because the equivalent proposition, or the other name for the remedy, sounds much less attractive, that the original proposal is under all conditions unsound. There may be times when an increase in debt is a minor consideration as against the gains achieved with the borrowed funds; when a government subsidy is unavoidable to achieve a certain military purpose; when a given industry can afford an increase in production costs, and so on. But we ought to make sure in each case that both sides of the coin have been considered, that all the implications of a proposal have been studied. And this is seldom done.

2

The analysis of our illustrations has taught us another incidental lesson. This is that, when we study the effects of various proposals, not merely on special groups in the short run, but on all groups in the long run, the conclusions we arrive at usually correspond with those of unsophisticated common sense. It would not occur to anyone unacquainted with the prevailing economic half-literacy that it is good to have windows broken and cities destroyed; that it is anything but waste to create needless public projects; that it is dangerous to let idle hordes of men return to work; that machines which increase the production of wealth and economize human effort are to be dreaded; that obstructions to free production and free consumption increase wealth; that a nation grows richer by forcing other nations to take its goods for less than they cost to produce; that saving is stupid or wicked and that squandering brings prosperity.

"What is prudence in the conduct of every private family," said Adam Smith's strong common sense in reply to the sophists of his time, "can scarce be folly in that of a great kingdom." But lesser men get lost in complications. They do not reexamine their reasoning even when they emerge with conclusions that are palpably absurd. The reader, depending upon his own beliefs, may or may not accept the aphorism of Bacon that "A little philosophy inclineth men's minds to atheism, but depth in philosophy bringeth men's minds about to religion." It is certainly true, however, that a little economics can easily lead to the paradoxical and preposterous conclusions we have just rehearsed, but that depth in economics brings men back to common sense. For depth in economics consists in looking for all the consequences of a policy instead of merely resting one's gaze on those immediately visible.

3

In the course of our study, also, we have rediscovered an old friend. He is the Forgotten Man of William Graham Sumner. The reader will remember that in Sumner's essay, which appeared in 1883:

> As soon as A observes something which seems to him to be wrong, from which X is suffering, A talks it over with B, and A and B then propose to get a law passed to remedy the evil and help X. Their law always proposes to determine what C shall do for X or, in the better case, what A, B and C shall do for X. . . . What I want to do

is to look up C. . . . I call him the Forgotten Man. . . . He is the man who never is thought of. He is the victim of the reformer, social speculator and philanthropist, and I hope to show you before I get through that he deserves your notice both for his character and for the many burdens which are laid upon him.

It is a historic irony that when this phrase, the Forgotten Man, was revived in the 1930s, it was applied, not to C, but to X; and C, who was then being asked to support still more Xs, was more completely forgotten than ever. It is C, the Forgotten Man, who is always called upon to stanch the politician's bleeding heart by paying for his vicarious generosity.

4

Our study of our lesson would not be complete if, before we took leave of it, we neglected to observe that the fundamental fallacy with which we have been concerned arises not accidentally but systematically. It is an almost inevitable result, in fact, of the division of labor.

In a primitive community, or among pioneers, before the division of labor has arisen, a man works solely for himself or his immediate family. What he consumes is identical with what he produces. There is always a direct and immediate connection between his output and his satisfactions.

But when an elaborate and minute division of labor has set in, this direct and immediate connection ceases to exist. I do not make all the things I consume but, perhaps, only one of them. With the income I derive from making this one commodity, or rendering this one service, I buy all the rest. I wish the price of everything I buy to be low, but it is in my interest for the price of the commodity or services that I have to sell to be high. Therefore, though I wish to see abundance in everything else, it is in my interest for scarcity to exist in the very thing that it is my business to supply. The greater the scarcity, compared to everything else, in this one thing that I supply, the higher will be the reward that I can get for my efforts.

This does not necessarily mean that I will restrict my own efforts or my own output. In fact, if I am only one of a substantial number of people supplying that commodity or service, and if free competition exists in my line, this individual restriction will not pay me. On the contrary, if I am a grower of wheat, say, I want my particular crop to be as large as possible. But if I am concerned only with my own material welfare, and have no humanitarian scruples, I want the output of all *other* wheat growers to be as *low* as possible; for I want scarcity in wheat (and in any foodstuff that can be substituted for it) so that my particular crop may command the highest possible price.

Ordinarily these selfish feelings would have no effect on the total production of wheat. Wherever competition exists, in fact, each producer is compelled to put forth his utmost efforts to raise the highest possible crop on his own land. In this way the forces of self-interest (which, for good or evil, are more persistently powerful than those of altruism) are harnessed to maximum output.

But if it is possible for wheat growers or any other group of producers to combine to eliminate competition, and if the government permits or encourages such a course, the situation changes. The wheat growers may be able to persuade the national government—or, better, a world organization—to force all of them to reduce pro rata the acreage planted to wheat. In this way they will bring about a shortage and raise the price of wheat; and if the rise in the price per bushel is proportionately greater, as it well may be, than the reduction in output, then the wheat growers as a whole will be better off. They will get more money; they will be able to buy more of everything else. Everybody else, it is true, will be worse off: because, other things equal, everyone else will have to give more of what he produces to get less of what the wheat grower produces. So the nation as a whole will be just that much poorer. It will be poorer by the amount of wheat that has not been grown. But those who look only at the wheat farmers will see a gain, and miss the more than offsetting loss.

And this applies in every other line. If because of unusual weather conditions there is a sudden increase in the crop of oranges, all the consumers will benefit. The world will be richer by that many more oranges. Oranges will be cheaper. But that very fact may make the orange growers as a group poorer than before, unless the greater supply of oranges compensates or more than compensates for the lower price. Certainly if under such conditions my particular crop of oranges is no larger than usual, then I am certain to lose by the lower price brought about by general plenty.

And what applies to changes in supply applies to changes in demand, whether brought about by new inventions and discoveries or by changes in taste. A new cotton-picking machine, though it may reduce the cost of cotton underwear and shirts to everyone, and increase the general wealth, will mean the employment of fewer cotton pickers. A new textile machine, weaving a better cloth at a faster rate, will make thousands of old machines obsolete, and wipe out part of the capital value invested in them, so making poorer the owners of those machines. The further development of nuclear power, though it can confer unimaginable blessings on mankind, is something that is dreaded by the owners of coal mines and oil wells.

Just as there is no technical improvement that would not hurt someone, so there is no change in public taste or morals, even for the better, that would not hurt someone. An increase in sobriety would put thousands of bartenders out of business. A decline in gambling would force croupiers and racing touts to seek more productive occupations. A growth of male chastity would ruin the oldest profession in the world.

But it is not merely those who deliberately pander to men's vices who would be hurt by a sudden improvement in public morals. Among those who would be hurt most are precisely those whose business it is to improve those morals. Preachers would have less to complain about; reformers would lose their causes; the demand for their services and contributions for their support would decline. If there were no criminals we should need fewer lawyers, judges and firemen, and no jailers, no locksmiths, and (except for such services as untangling traffic snarls) even no policemen.

Under a system of division of labor, in short, it is difficult to think of a greater fulfillment of any human need which would not, at least temporarily, hurt some of the people who have made investments or painfully acquired skill to meet that precise need. If progress were completely even all around the circle, this antagonism between the interests of the whole community and of the specialized group would not, if it were noticed at all, present any serious problem. If in the same year as the world wheat crop increased, my own crop increased in the same proportion, if the crop of oranges and all other agricultural products increased correspondingly, and if the output of all industrial goods also rose and their unit cost of production fell to correspond, then I as a wheat grower would not suffer because the output of wheat had increased. The price that I got for a bushel of wheat might decline. The total sum that I realized from my larger output might decline. But if I could also because of increased supplies buy the output of everyone else cheaper, then I should have no real cause to complain. If the price of everything else dropped in exactly the same ratio as the decline in the price of my wheat, I should be better off, in fact, exactly in proportion to my increased total crop; and everyone else, likewise, would benefit proportionately from the in creased supplies of all goods and services.

But economic progress never has taken place and probably never will take place in this completely uniform way. Advance occurs now in this branch of production and now in that. And if there is a sudden increase in the supply of the thing I help to produce, or if a new invention or discovery makes what I produce no longer necessary, then the gain to the world is a tragedy to me and to the productive group to which I belong.

Now it is often not the diffused gain of the increased supply or new discovery that most forcibly strikes even the disinterested observer, but the concentrated loss. The fact that there is more and cheaper coffee for everyone is lost sight of; what is seen is merely that some coffee growers cannot make a living at the lower price.

The increased output of shoes at lower cost by the new machine is forgotten; what is seen is a group of men and women thrown out of work. It is altogether proper—it is, in fact, essential to a full understanding of the problem—that the plight of these groups be recognized, that they be dealt with sympathetically, and that we try to see whether some of the gains from this specialized progress cannot be used to help the victims find a productive role elsewhere.

But the solution is never to reduce supplies arbitrarily, to prevent further inventions or discoveries, or to support people for continuing to perform a service that has lost its value. Yet this is what the world has repeatedly sought to do by protective tariffs, by the destruction of machinery, by the burning of coffee, by a thousand restriction schemes. This is the insane doctrine of wealth through scarcity.

It is a doctrine that may always be privately true, unfortunately, for any particular group of producers considered in isolation—if they can make scarce the one thing they have to sell while keeping abundant all the things they have to buy. But it is a doctrine that is always publicly false. It can never be applied all around the circle. For its application would mean economic suicide.

And this is our lesson in its most generalized form. For many things that seem to be true when we concentrate on a single economic group are seen to be illusions when the interests of everyone, as consumer no less than as producer, are considered.

To see the problem as a whole, and not in fragments: that is the goal of economic science.

Part Three

The Lesson After Thirty Years

CHAPTER XXVI

The Lesson after Thirty Years

THE FIRST EDITION of this book appeared in 1946. It is now, as I write this, thirty-two years later. How much of the lesson expounded in the previous pages has been learned in this period?

If we are referring to the politicians—to all those responsible for formulating and imposing government policies—practically none of it has been learned. On the contrary, the policies analyzed in the preceding chapters are far more deeply established and widespread, not only in the United States, but in practically every country in the world, than they were when this book first appeared.

We may take, as the outstanding example, inflation. This is not only a policy imposed for its own sake, but an inevitable result of most of the other interventionist policies. It stands today as the universal symbol of government intervention everywhere.

The 1946 edition explained the consequences of inflation, but the inflation then was comparatively mild. True, though federal government expenditures in 1926 had been less than $3 billion and there was a surplus, by fiscal year 1946 expenditures had risen to $55 billion and there was a deficit of $16 billion. Yet in fiscal year 1947, with the war ended, expenditures fell to $35 billion and there was an actual surplus of nearly $4 billion. By fiscal year 1978, however, expenditures had soared to $451 billion and the deficit to $49 billion.

All this has been accompanied by an enormous increase in the stock of money—from $113 billion of demand deposits plus currency outside of banks in 1947, to $357 billion in August 1978. In other words, the active money supply has been more than tripled in the period.

The effect of this increase in money has been a dramatic increase in prices. The consumer price index in 1946 stood at 58.5. In September 1978 it was 199.3. Prices, in short, more than tripled.[12]

The policy of inflation, as I have said, is partly imposed for its own sake. More than forty years after the publication of John Maynard Keynes' *General Theory*, and more than twenty years after that book has been thoroughly discredited by analysis and experience, a great number of our politicians are still unceasingly recommending more deficit spending in order to cure or reduce existing unemployment. An appalling irony is that they are making these recommendations when the federal government has already been running a deficit for forty-one out of the last forty-eight years and when that deficit has been reaching dimensions of $50 billion a year.[13]

An even greater irony is that, not satisfied with following such disastrous policies at home, our officials have been scolding other countries, notably Germany and Japan, for not following these "expansionary" policies themselves. This reminds one of nothing so much as Aesop's fox, who, when he had lost his tail, urged all his fellow foxes to cut off theirs.

One of the worst results of the retention of the Keynesian myths is that it not only promotes greater and greater inflation, but that it systematically diverts attention from the real causes of our unemployment, such as excessive union wage-rates, minimum wage laws, excessive and prolonged unemployment insurance, and overgenerous relief payments.

But the inflation, though in part often deliberate, is today mainly the consequence of other government economic interventions. It is the consequence, in brief, of the Redistributive State — of all the policies of expropriating money from Peter in order to lavish it on Paul.

This process would be easier to trace, and its ruinous effects easier to expose, if it were all done in some single measure — like the guaranteed annual income actually proposed and seriously considered by committees of Congress in the early 1970s. This was a proposal to tax still more ruthlessly all incomes above average and turn the proceeds over to all those living below a so-called minimum poverty line, in order to guarantee them an income—whether they were willing to work or not—"to enable them to live with dignity." It would be hard to imagine a plan more clearly calculated to discourage work and production and eventually to impoverish everybody.

But instead of passing any such single measure, and bringing on ruin in a single swoop, our government has preferred to enact a hundred laws that effect such a redistribution on a partial and selective basis. These measures may miss some needy groups entirely; but on the other hand they may shower upon other groups a dozen different varieties of benefits, subsidies, and other hand-outs. These include, to give a random list: Social Security, Medicare, Medicaid, unemployment insurance, food stamps, veterans' benefits, farm subsidies, subsidized housing, rent subsidies, school lunches, public employment on make-work jobs, Aid to Families with Dependent Children, and direct relief of all kinds, including aid to the aged, the blind, and the disabled. The federal government has estimated that under these last categories it has been handing federal aid benefits to more than 4 million people—not to count what the states and cities are doing.

One author has recently counted and examined no fewer than forty-four welfare programs. Government expenditures for these in 1976 totaled $187 billion. The combined average growth of these programs between 1971 and 1976 was 25 percent a year—2.5 times the rate of growth of estimated gross national product for the same period. Projected expenditures for 1979 are more than $250 billion. Coincident with the extraordinary growth of these welfare expenditures has been the development of a "national welfare industry," now composed of 5 million public and private workers distributing payments and services to 50 million beneficiaries.[*]

---

[*] Charles D. Hobbs, *The Welfare Industry* (Washington, D.C.: Heritage Foundation, 1978).

Nearly every other Western country has been administering a similar assortment of aid programs—though sometimes a more integrated and less haphazard collection. And in order to do this they have been resorting to more and more Draconian taxation.

We need merely point to Great Britain as one example. Its government has been taxing personal income from work ("earned" income) up to 83 percent, and personal income from investment ("unearned" income) up to 98 percent. Should it be surprising that it has discouraged work and investment and so profoundly discouraged production and employment? There is no more certain way to deter employment than to harass and penalize employers. There is no more certain way to keep wages low than to destroy every incentive to investment in new and more efficient machines and equipment. But this is becoming more and more the policy of governments everywhere.[14]

Yet this Draconian taxation has not brought revenues to keep pace with ever more reckless government spending and schemes for redistributing wealth. The result has been to bring chronic and growing government budget deficits, and therefore chronic and mounting inflation, in nearly every country in the world.

For the last thirty years or so, Citibank of New York has been keeping a record of this inflation over ten-year periods. Its calculations are based on the cost-of-living estimates published by the individual governments themselves. In its economic letter of October 1977 it published a survey of inflation in fifty countries. These figures show that in 1976, for example, the West German mark, with the best record, had lost 35 percent of its purchasing power over the preceding ten years; that the Swiss franc had lost 40 percent, the American dollar 43 percent, the French franc 50 percent, the Japanese yen 57 percent, the Swedish krone 47 percent, the Italian lira 56 percent, and the British pound 61 percent. When we get to Latin America, the Brazilian cruzeiro had lost 89 percent of its value, and the Uruguayan, Chilean, and Argentine pesos more than 99 percent.

Though when compared with the record of a year or two before, the overall record of world currency depreciations was more moderate; the American dollar in 1977 was depreciating at an annual rate of 6 percent, the French franc of 8.6 percent, the Japanese yen of 9.1 percent, the Swedish krone of 9.5 percent, the British pound of 14.5 percent, the Italian lira of 15.7 percent, and the Spanish peseta at an annual rate of 17.5 percent. As for Latin American experience, the Brazilian currency unit in 1977 was depreciating at an *annual* rate of 30.8 percent, the Uruguayan of 35.5, the Chilean of 53.9, and the Argentinian of 65.7.[15]

I leave it to the reader to picture the chaos that these rates of depreciation of money were producing in the economies of these countries and the suffering in the lives of millions of their inhabitants.

As I have pointed out, these inflations, themselves the cause of so much human misery, were in turn in large part the consequence of other policies of government economic intervention. Practically all these interventions unintentionally illustrate and underline the basic lesson of this book. All were enacted on the assumption that they would confer some immediate benefit on some special group. Those who enacted them failed to take heed of their secondary consequences—failed to consider what their effect would be in the long run on all groups.

In sum, so far as the politicians are concerned, the lesson that this book tried to instill more than thirty years ago does not seem to have been learned anywhere.

If we go through the chapters of this book seriatim, we find practically no form of government intervention deprecated in the first edition that is not still being pursued, usually with increased obstinacy. Governments everywhere are still trying to cure by public works the unemployment brought about by their own policies. They are imposing heavier and more expropriatory taxes than ever. They still recommend credit expansion. Most of them still make "full employment" their overriding goal. They continue to impose import quotas and protective tariffs. They try to increase exports by depreciating their currencies even further. Farmers are still "striking" for "parity prices." Governments still provide special encouragements to unprofitable industries. They still make efforts to "stabilize" special commodity prices.

Governments, pushing up commodity prices by inflating their currencies, continue to blame the higher prices on private producers, sellers, and "profiteers." They impose price ceilings on oil and natural gas, to discourage new exploration precisely when it is in most need of encouragement, or resort to general price and wage fixing or "monitoring." They continue rent control in the face of the obvious devastation it has caused. They not only retain minimum wage laws but keep increasing their level, in face of the chronic unemployment they so clearly bring about. They continue to pass laws granting special privileges and immunities to labor unions; to oblige workers to become members; to tolerate mass picketing and other forms of coercion; and to compel employers to "bargain collectively in good faith" with such unions — i.e., to make at least some concessions to their demands. The intention of all these measures is to "help labor." But the result is once more to create and prolong unemployment, and to lower total wage payments compared with what they might have been.

Most politicians continue to ignore the necessity of profits, to overestimate their average or total net amount, to denounce unusual profits anywhere, to tax them excessively, and sometimes even to deplore the very existence of profits.

The anticapitalistic mentality seems more deeply embedded than ever. Whenever there is any slowdown in business, the politicians now see the main cause as "insufficient consumer spending." At the same time that they encourage more consumer spending they pile up further disincentives and penalties in the way of saving and investment. Their chief method of doing this today, as we have already seen, is to embark on or accelerate inflation. The result is that today, for the first time in history, no nation is on a metallic standard, and practically every nation is swindling its own people by printing a chronically depreciating paper currency.

To pile one more item on this heap, let us examine the recent tendency, not only in the United States but abroad, for almost every "social" program, once launched upon, to get completely out of hand. We have already glanced at the overall picture, but let us now look more closely at one outstanding example—Social Security in the United States.

The original federal Social Security Act was passed in 1935. The theory behind it was that the greater part of the relief problem was that people did not save in their working years, and so, when they were too old to work, they found themselves without resources. This problem could be solved, it was thought, if they were compelled to insure themselves, with employers also compelled to contribute half the necessary premiums, so that they would have a pension sufficient to retire on at age sixty-five or over. Social Security was to be entirely a self-financed insurance plan based on strict actuarial principles. A reserve fund was to be set up sufficient to meet future claims and payments as they fell due.

It never worked out that way. The reserve fund existed mainly on paper. The government spent the Social Security tax receipts, as they came in, either to meet its ordinary expenses or to pay out benefits. Since 1975, current benefit payments have exceeded the system's tax receipts.

It also turned out that in practically every session Congress found ways to increase the benefits paid, broaden the coverage, and add new forms of "social insurance." As one commentator pointed out in 1965, a few weeks after Medicare insurance was added: "Social Security sweeteners have been enacted in each of the past seven general election years."

As inflation developed and progressed, Social Security benefits were increased not only in proportion, but much more. The typical political ploy was to load up benefits in the present and push costs into the future. Yet that future always arrived; and each few years later Congress would again have to increase payroll taxes levied on both workers and employers.

Not only were the tax rates continuously increased, but there was a constant rise in the amount of salary taxed. In the original 1935 bill the salary taxed was only the first $3,000. The early tax rates were very low. But between 1965 and 1977, for example, the

Social Security tax shot up from 4.4 percent on the first $6,600 of earned income (levied on employer and employee alike) to a combined 11.7 percent on the first $16,500. (Between 1960 and 1977, the total annual tax increased by 572 percent, or about 12 percent a year compounded. It is scheduled to go much higher.)

At the beginning of 1977, unfunded liabilities of the Social Security system were officially estimated at $4.1 *trillion*.[16]

No one can say today whether Social Security is really an insurance program or just a complicated and lopsided relief system. The bulk of the present benefit recipients are being assured that they "earned" and "paid for" their benefits. Yet no private insurance company could have afforded to pay existing benefit scales out of the "premiums" actually received. As of early 1978, when low-paid workers retire, their monthly benefits generally represent about 60 percent of what they earned on the job. Middle-income workers receive about 45 percent. For those with exceptionally high salaries, the ratio can fall to 5 or 10 percent. If Social Security is thought of as a relief system, however, it is a very strange one, for those who have already been getting the highest salaries receive the highest dollar benefits.

Yet Social Security today is still sacrosanct. It is considered political suicide for any congressman to suggest cutting down or cutting back not only present but promised future benefits. The American Social Security system must stand today as a frightening symbol of the almost inevitable tendency of any national relief, redistribution, or "insurance" scheme, once established, to run completely out of control.

In brief, the main problem we face today is not economic, but political. Sound economists are in substantial agreement concerning what ought to be done. Practically all government attempts to redistribute wealth and income tend to smother productive incentives and lead toward general impoverishment. It is the proper sphere of government to create and enforce a framework of law that prohibits force and fraud. But it must refrain from specific economic interventions. Government's main economic function is to encourage and preserve a free market. When Alexander the

Great visited the philosopher Diogenes and asked whether he could do anything for him, Diogenes is said to have replied: "Yes, stand a little less between me and the sun." It is what every citizen is entitled to ask of his government.

The outlook is dark, but it is not entirely without hope. Here and there one can detect a break in the clouds. More and more people are becoming aware that government has nothing to give them without first taking it away from somebody else—or from themselves. Increased handouts to selected groups mean merely increased taxes, or increased deficits and increased inflation. And inflation, in the end, misdirects and disorganizes production. Even a few politicians are beginning to recognize this, and some of them even to state it clearly.

In addition, there are marked signs of a shift in the intellectual winds of doctrine. Keynesians and New Dealers seem to be in a slow retreat. Conservatives, libertarians, and other defenders of free enterprise are becoming more outspoken and more articulate. And there are many more of them. Among the young, there is a rapid growth of a disciplined school of "Austrian" economists.

There is a real promise that public policy may be reversed before the damage from existing measures and trends has become irreparable.

A Note On Books

THOSE WHO DESIRE to read further in economics should turn next to some work of intermediate length and difficulty. I know of no single volume in print today that completely meets this need, but there are several that together supply it. There is an excellent short book (126 pages) by Faustino Ballvé, *Essentials of Economics* (Irvington-on-Hudson, N.Y.: Foundation for Economic Education), which briefly summarizes principles and policies. A book that does that at somewhat greater length (327 pages) is *Understanding the Dollar Crisis* by Percy L. Greaves (Belmont, Mass.: Western Islands, 1973). Bettina Bien Greaves has assembled two volumes of readings on *Free Market Economics* (Foundation for Economic Education).

The reader who aims at a thorough understanding, and feels prepared for it, should next read *Human Action* by Ludwig von Mises (Chicago: Contemporary Books, 1949, 1966, 907 pages). This book extended the logical unity and precision of economics beyond that of any previous work. A two-volume work written thirteen years after *Human Action* by a student of Mises is Murray N. Rothbard's *Man, Economy, and State* (Mission, Kan.: Sheed, Andrews and McMeel, 1962, 987 pages). This contains much original and penetrating material; its exposition is admirably lucid; and its arrangement makes it in some respects more suitable for textbook use than Mises' great work.

Short books that discuss special economic subjects in a simple way are *Planning for Freedom* by Ludwig von Mises (South Holland, Ill.: Libertarian Press, 1952), and *Capitalism and Freedom* by Milton Friedman (Chicago: University of Chicago Press, 1962).

There is an excellent pamphlet by Murray N. Rothbard, *What Has Government Done to Our Money?* (Santa Ana, Calif.: Rampart College, 1964, 1974, 62 pages). On the urgent subject of inflation, a book by the present author has recently been published, *The Inflation Crisis, and How to Resolve It* (New Rochelle, N.Y.: Arlington House, 1978).

Among recent works which discuss current ideologies and developments from a point of view similar to that of this volume are the present author's *The Failure of the "New Economics": An Analysis of the Keynesian Fallacies* (Arlington House, 1959); F. A. Hayek, *The Road to Serfdom* (1945) and the same author's monumental *Constitution of Liberty* (Chicago: University of Chicago Press, 1960). Ludwig von Mises' *Socialism: An Economic and Sociological Analysis* (London: Jonathan Cape, 1936, 1969) is the most thorough and devastating critique of collectivistic doctrines ever written.

The reader should not overlook, of course, Frederic Bastiat's *Economic Sophisms* (*ca.* 1844), and particularly his essay on "What Is Seen and What Is Not Seen."

Those who are interested in working through the economic classics might find it most profitable to do this in the reverse of their historical order. Presented in this order, the chief works to be consulted, with the dates of their first editions, are: Philip Wicksteed, *The Common Sense of Political Economy*, 1911; John Bates Clark, *The Distribution of Wealth*, 1899; Eugen von Böhm-Bawerk, The Positive Theory of Capital, 1888; Karl Menger, *Principles of Economics*, 1871; W. Stanley Jevons, *The Theory of Political Economy*, 1871; John Stuart Mill, *Principles of Political Economy*, 1848; David Ricardo, *Principles of Political Economy and Taxation*, 1817; and Adam Smith, *The Wealth of Nations*, 1776.

Economics broadens out in a hundred directions. Whole libraries have been written on specialized fields alone, such as money and banking, foreign trade and foreign exchange, taxation and public finance, government control, capitalism and socialism, wages and labor relations, interest and capital, agricultural economics, rent, prices, profits, markets, competition and monopoly, value and utility, statistics, business cycles, wealth and poverty, social insurance, housing, public utilities, mathematical economics, studies of special industries and of economic history. But no one will ever properly understand any of these specialized fields unless he has first of all acquired a firm grasp of basic economic principles and the complex interrelationship of all economic factors and forces. When he has done this by his reading in general economics, he can be trusted to find the right books in his special field of interest.

ENDNOTES [*]

1. National income was $6.2 trillion in 1989 (1993 dollars). Taxes equalled $2.4 trillion, or approximately 40% of the national income. ("What is the Optimal Size of Government?" Gerald W. Scully, NCPA Report No. 188, November 1994.)

2. In a 1992 essay written for the Dallas Federal Reserve Bank by economists W. Michael Cox and Richard Alm, the authors point out the constant process of job creation. Economist Joseph Schumpeter first recognized this "creative destruction," whereby technological innovation creates new job opportunities as it frees up labor from old jobs. Cox and Alm explore the explosive growth of employment in this century from 29,000,000 U.S. workers in 1900 to 116,000,000 in 1991. ("The Churn," W. Michael Cox and Richard Alm, Federal Reserve Board of Dallas Annual Report, 1992.)

3. The $5,000 figure Hazlitt uses is not meant to be exact. The average price of a new car now borders on $20,000. ("Fun and Games With Inflation," David R. Henderson, *Fortune*, March 18, 1996, p. 36.)

4. The situation has not gotten better since Hazlitt added the footnote. According to *Investor's Business Daily* (September 29, 1995), "From 1986 through 1993, the cotton program's costs totaled $12 billion and averaged $1.5 billion a year. And like many farm programs, large payments went to a small number of producers. In 1993, just under 96,000 growers divvied up the proceeds." The additional costs to consumers are also high. According to a GAO study released July 20, 1995, the program cost society $738 million on average each year for

---

[*] Our thanks to Philip Michelbach of the Free Enterprise Institute for providing these updated statistics.

the previous eight years. The same GAO report concluded that "the cotton program has evolved into a costly, complex maze of domestic and international price supports that benefit cotton producers at the cost of government and society." Attempts by the 104th Congress to reform this program have failed.

5. The minimum wage is now $4.25 an hour. A forty-hour week based on this wage costs an employer $170 in wages alone.

6. Since Hazlitt added the footnote, the minimum wage has been increased three times: in 1981 it was increased to $3.35, in 1990 to $3.80, and in 1992 to $4.25. Increases in unemployment (especially teenage minority unemployment) and decreases in job creation followed each of these increases. ("Should the Federal Minimum Wage Be Increased?" Richard Vedder and Lowell Gallaway, NCPA Policy Report No. 190, February 1995.)

7. The percentage of the labor force now unionized is 15.5%. (*Investor's Business Daily*, November 14, 1995.)

8. Compensation as a percentage of national output has remained fairly constant at about 60% over the past forty years, reported *Investor's Business Daily*, January 4, 1996. Economist Kenneth P. Voytek reports that hourly non-farm compensation increased 2.4% annually from 1959–1972. Annual growth in compensation slowed to .8% from 1973–1994. This was due to increased productivity which averaged 2.4% from 1959–1972, but only 1% from 1973–1994. Overall, compensation as a percentage of national income has increased about 4% since 1959, while union membership dropped precipitously. Increases are often in non-wage compensation like health-care and job training. (*Investor's Business Daily*, January 8, 1996.)

9. For more current figures on wages and salaries as a percentage of national income, see 8 above.

10. According to economist Kenneth P. Voytek, before-tax corporate profits averaged 10–12% during the 1960s and 1970s. They declined to less than 8% during the 1980s and have risen to around 9% in the 1990s. (*Investor's Business Daily*, January 8, 1996.)

11. For more current figures on corporate profits, see 10 above.

12. Economist David R. Henderson reports that "in the 56 years since 1939, inflation has averaged 4.4% a year. Although that sounds small,

even moderate inflation adds up over time. Actually, it doesn't add up. It multiplies up. Inflation, like interest, compounds. Net result: Since 1939, prices have increased 998%." ("Fun and Games with Inflation," David R. Henderson, *Fortune*, March 18, 1996, p. 35.)

13. By 1992 the budget deficit had reached $290 billion. Since then the shortfall declined to "only" $165 billion in 1995. (*Investor's Business Daily*, October 5, 1995.)

14. Great Britain had a 40% top tax rate on income, a 17.5% VAT, and a 33% capital gains tax. (*1996 Index of Economic Freedom*, Brian T. Johnson and Thomas P. Sheehy, The Heritage Foundation, 1996.) Taxes absorbed 34% of GNP in 1994. (*The Economist*, February 9, 1995, p. 99.)

15. Annual inflation rates for various countries' currencies in 1994: USA 2.8%, France 1.7%, Japan -2%, Sweden 4.5%, UK 2.4%, Italy 4%, Spain 4.5%, Brazil 2,500%, Uruguay 40%, Chile 11%, Argentina 5%. (*1996 Index of Economic Freedom*, Brian T. Johnson and Thomas P. Sheehy, The Heritage Foundation, 1996.)

16. The Social Security tax rate is now 15.3%. It is estimated that the program will become insolvent in 2010.

Index

If you enjoyed this book and would like to
see more of the literature of liberty, call us at

877 - 453 - 1177

or write to us at

Laissez Faire Books
808 St. Paul Street
Baltimore, MD. 21202

Quantity discounts available.